Learn
MYOB
in 7 DAYS

T0311057

Learn
MYOB
in 7 DAYS

TURBO BOOST YOUR BUSINESS

HEATHER SMITH

Wrightbooks

First published in 2012 by Wrightbooks
an imprint of John Wiley & Sons Australia, Ltd
42 McDougall St, Milton Qld 4064

Office also in Melbourne

Typeset in 11.5/14.3 Berkeley LT Book

© Heather Smith 2012

The moral rights of the author have been asserted.

National Library of Australia Cataloguing-in-Publication data:

Author:	Smith, Heather (Heather Nicolette)
Title:	Learn MYOB in 7 days: turbo boost your business / Heather Smith.
ISBN:	9780730375920 (pbk.)
Notes:	Includes index.
Subjects:	M.Y.O.B. (Computer program) Accounting—Australia—Computer programs—Handbooks, manuals, etc. Small business—Accounting—Computer programs—Handbooks, manuals, etc.
Dewey Number:	657.0285536

All rights reserved. Except as permitted under the *Australian Copyright Act 1968* (for example, a fair dealing for the purposes of study, research, criticism or review), no part of this book may be reproduced, stored in a retrieval system, communicated or transmitted in any form or by any means without prior written permission. All inquiries should be made to the publisher at the address above.

Cover design by Xou Creative

Screen captures from MYOB reproduced with permission. Copyright © 2011 MYOB Technology Pty Ltd. MYOB® is a registered trademark of MYOB Technology Pty Ltd and its affiliates.

Printed in Australia by Ligare Book Printer

10 9 8 7 6 5 4 3 2 1

Disclaimer

The material in this publication is of the nature of general comment only, and does not represent professional advice. It is not intended to provide specific guidance for particular circumstances and it should not be relied on as the basis for any decision to take action or not take action on any matter which it covers. Readers should obtain professional advice where appropriate, before making any such decision. To the maximum extent permitted by law, the author and publisher disclaim all responsibility and liability to any person, arising directly or indirectly from any person taking or not taking action based on the information in this publication.

Contents

About the author

Heather Smith has always had a particular interest in the workings of small business and is passionate about helping small business owners understand their numbers to enable them to maximise their productivity and profitability. She utilises remote technology to connect with the businesses computer and is able to provide education, training and support across Australia.

She writes for national online and printed publications, including *The Daily Telegraph*, Flying Solo (a website for 'solopreneurs'), My Business (a website for business advice), ninemsn, *Woman's Day*, *Courier Mail*, *Latte* and *Network* magazine.

She has a bachelor of commerce from Griffith University in Queensland and is a Chartered Accountant and a Fellow and an Ambassador of the Association of Chartered Certified Accountants (ACCA). Heather is an MYOB Certified Consultant, an MYOB Specialist Trainer, an MYOB Accredited Author and a XERO and SAASU consultant.

Heather is in demand on the speaking circuit, and her presentations on a range of small business topics never fail to excite and inspire her audiences.

> 'The world of small business needs more people like Heather.'
>
> *Robert Gerrish, founder and director of Flying Solo*

Heather has enthusiastically embraced the world of technology and social media, and uses both to help her connect with small business people and to understand their most pressing issues. Heather is currently working on her next book, *Learn Small Business Start-up in 7 Days*.

Be part of the action by connecting with Heather:

▶ Website: <www.learnMYOBin7days.com>

▶ LinkedIn: <www.linkedin.com/in/MYOBTrainer>

▶ Twitter: @HeatherSmithAU

Acknowledgements

I have always loved to write and create stories. I have always dreamt of being an author, but never really thought that it would become a reality, nor that my first book would be a business software book. I am so grateful to Kristen Hammond, Annette Sayers and the team at John Wiley & Sons Australia, Ltd—thank you for taking a chance on me.

Thank you to Sam Leader, Robert Gerrish and Peter Crocker, and everyone associated with Flying Solo, especially Amanda Gonzalez, Kate Tribe and Lucinda Lions, who have provided me with a bottomless cup of support. Special thanks to Sam Leader, the editor at Flying Solo, who rejected my first submission—and made me want it more and try harder.

Many thanks to Craig Winkler, who launched MYOB here in Australia. I truly believe that MYOB has contributed to the success of many businesses in Australia and beyond. Thank you to the team at MYOB and my fellow consultants, and special thanks to Simon McCormack, the best account manager a consultant could ever have. Thank you to Julian Smith, Rick Van Dyk and Wayne Schmidt, who are always available for a thoughtful chat, no matter who they are working for! A huge thank you to all my clients, who have taken this journey with me. Special thanks to Ken, my very first client, for having faith in me, and to his lovely wife, Sue, who ensures that I have lots of cups of tea and bickies when I visit.

Thank you to Letitia Alder, my first accounting teacher, who introduced me to the magic of debits and credits.

Thank you to Valerie Khoo and the team at the Sydney Writers Centre. Thank you, Valerie, for being so accessible and so generous in sharing your knowledge. I feel that I have learned more from you about the skill and art of writing than from the many years I spent within institutional learning environments.

Thank you to Andrew Griffiths, Mel Kettle, Karen Smith and Adam Wallace, who have taken time out of their busy lives to help me brainstorm the future.

Thank you to my fellow members of the Australian Institute of Management Queensland lunchtime speaking group, and to Lisa and the Bulimba Riverside Toastmasters, who have evaluated the many talks that I have been able to incorporate in this book. Thank you to Axiom College, who first let me loose on unsuspecting MYOB students.

To my Mum and Dad, family and friends—thank you. To the best friends a girl could have, Bridget, Tania and Sharron—thank you.

To my raison d'être, my children—everything in my world revolves around you, Christopher and Charlotte, thank you for just being you and making me so proud every day. Thank you to my dog, Charlie, who has sat at my feet for endless hours and every so often drops a ball at my feet, knowing I need to take a break and encouraging me to get away from the desk and into the backyard for a play. Finally, *muchas gracias* to my husband, Simon. Words cannot express how grateful, how lucky and how fortunate I am to have you in my life: xxx.

Introduction

Over the years I have trained thousands of people in the use of Mind Your Own Business (MYOB) business management software, ranging from how to do simple basic data entry and perform bank reconciliations to how to prepare Business Activity Statements (BAS) and manage business accounting records. This book is a crash course in MYOB. It explains the basics of MYOB in a way that is simple to understand. Some people intuitively 'get' MYOB and run with it; others take longer to master this software. I understand that MYOB can cause some people a lot of stress, because it involves working with numbers, with financials and with computers, and for this reason it can seem daunting and frustrating.

In this book we are going to work through the basics of MYOB step by step, building on your knowledge day by day and revising what you have learned along the way. To learn how to drive a car, you don't need to have a detailed understanding of the car's mechanics and electronics. Similarly, at the end of seven days you will not know everything there is to know about MYOB or bookkeeping, but you will be able to drive MYOB with confidence and know enough to be able to use it in a practical business environment.

Each reader will come to this book with a different level of experience. For example, you may have to set up a data file from scratch, or be required to work on an existing data file, and not know how to go about this; or you may be familiar with the basics of MYOB but want to learn more about the software's capabilities. We will cover all the basics in this book, including how to set up a data file, but readers with some experience of MYOB may wish to move ahead to a section that is more relevant to them. Personally, I go through every training manual I lay my hands on with a finetooth comb. I always find I learn something new—a timesaving trick, a different way to do something—and if I'm lucky I may experience a 'light bulb' moment.

You may think of MYOB as a single software program. In fact there is a wide range of MYOB software, each version offering different features to meet the needs of a variety of small business owners. You may be a microbusiness now, but if you have your sights set on world domination, it's worth considering what you will need your accounting system to do for you tomorrow. If you create a data file in MYOB Business Basics, you can upgrade to an MYOB product with more features as your business expands.

In this book I will be suggesting the simplest way to tackle accounts processing within MYOB. As a professional trainer and consultant, I come into contact with hundreds of different businesses, and it's my experience that some of them make life harder for themselves than it needs to be. It's critical to understand what information you want MYOB to generate before you start working with it. I also recommend that you always implement policies, procedures and rules on the assumption that the business is going to grow larger. For example, if you are processing employee mobile phone expenses for the month, do you process each employee individually or do you process the expenses as a total for the month? If the former, you should ask yourself whether a bulk entry would generate the same information and save you valuable time, especially as your business grows.

MYOB is currently the most popular accounting software and business management tool used by small businesses in Australia. Any time you spend learning this product is time well spent.

An overview of MYOB software in Australia

If you have not yet purchased your software, or if you feel that the software you are using is not meeting all your requirements, it's worth taking the time to read the next section. Choosing the right accounting software for your business can be difficult—and may even be critical to the ultimate success of your business—but there is no 'one size fits all' solution. Being a business owner, you need to consider what your individual requirements are for your business, both now and in the future.

MYOB business management software comes in many different shapes and sizes. The packages listed here are just a selection. This book will use MYOB AccountRight Plus in the examples, but the terminology, features and feel are the same across all the packages.

Business Basics

As the name suggests, Business Basics is the introductory MYOB software. While many of its features are similar to those found in the more sophisticated products on offer, Business

Basics is a simple program that is deliberately limited in scope. But don't underestimate this software — it can produce invoices, undertake bank reconciliations and generate more than 70 reports. Like all MYOB business accounting software, Business Basics complies with the requirements of the Australian Taxation Office (ATO). It can record goods and services tax (GST) and produce activity statements.

New owners of small businesses sometimes start off using Microsoft Excel spreadsheets, but this software has several drawbacks in this regard. Importantly, it is not designed to generate reports, and many accountants will charge you an additional fee to rework the data. Business Basics retails at under $300, and personally I really like this software. It does everything many soloists or start-up businesses need, at a modest cost, and it's a simple matter to upgrade it as the business grows.

AccountRight Standard

AccountRight Standard represents the next step up from Business Basics. It has all the features of Business Basics plus more extensive fields and reporting options within the areas of inventory management, purchasing and card files. Highlights of this package include the Company Data Auditor, which reviews the integrity of the data; the ability to synchronise contacts with Microsoft Outlook; and a feature called Business Insights Dashboard, which gives you a quick overview of the business's finances.

AccountRight Plus

The AccountRight Plus package has all the features of AccountRight Standard plus functions that allow you to manage time billing and, notably, payroll. The payroll function allows you to add employees, to maintain activity slips and time sheets, to process pay, to produce payment summaries, and also to create the annual summary of payroll information required by the ATO known as the EMPDUPE files. Using a computerised payroll system can be a major timesaver at the end of the payroll year. The latest Australian version of AccountRight Plus will have a feature that used to only be found in AccountRight Premier. The inventory module features a selling price matrix, which enables you to have multiple selling prices for an individual item.

AccountRight Premier

As your business grows and you require two or more people to access your MYOB software simultaneously, you can upgrade to AccountRight Premier. This is a networked version that allows up to three users to operate MYOB simultaneously. You can purchase additional user licences for this purpose. It's advisable to engage a networking expert to install your MYOB AccountRight software, as incorrect installation will affect the software's performance. AccountRight Premier has a couple of additional features. You can activate a multicurrency function that allows you to record import and export transactions in any foreign currency and to track realised and unrealised exchange gains and losses.

Choosing the right package

Over the years that I have worked in this field, I have seen many business owners struggling to work with packages that are wrong for them. They have either been oversold on features that they don't need or overwhelmed by unnecessary expense, or the package they are using simply doesn't meet their reporting requirements.

When you are investigating your options, here are the questions you need to ask:

▶ *Costs.* What are the upfront, ongoing and associated costs of the package? Typically, there will be the initial purchase cost plus the cost of installation. A rule of thumb when estimating a training budget is to allow the same amount as was spent on the purchase and installation of the software. There may also be annual upgrade costs; for example, to make full use of the payroll function in MYOB AccountRight Plus you must pay for new payroll tax tables every year. Hidden costs may include ongoing training, IT assistance, setting up a back-up system, and upgrading your computer and server hardware, depending on the size of your system.

▶ *Accountant preference.* What software does your accountant recommend? Is your accountant familiar with MYOB? (You do need to ask—don't just assume that he or she will be.) If so, does your accountant use the MYOB Accountants Office suite (the accountants' software for processing clients' MYOB files)? If not, your accountant may charge an additional fee to cover the cost of adapting your financial records to the system he or she uses.

▶ *Support.* What support is available when you have questions or need advice? Of all the accounting software products available in Australia, MYOB must be number one for support options. Within MYOB there are built in Help options, and online there are comprehensive support notes at <www.MYOB.com.au/supportnotes>. For a nominal subscription fee, MYOB Cover provides phone and instant chat support during office hours. The cherry on the cake is that MYOB has a team of

800 Certified Consultants across Australia and beyond for on-site support.

Navigating MYOB

Even software undergoes facelifts. MYOB software has dramatically changed its look recently. This book has been developed using the latest screenshots available. But if you plan to work though this book using an existing data file, or you are working in an environment where the MYOB screen looks different from what you see here, there is no need to stress. You will find that most things are essentially the same, and I will guide you through any major differences.

The PC-based software is covered in this book. There are three products available for Macs. Once you are within the Mac software, you will find that the orientation is very similar to that of the PC version. MYOB now offers online or cloud-based software called LiveAccounts, but this product is beyond the range of this book.

Essentially, your MYOB software is a database of information that intersects at various points to create a transaction. The database consists of many different types of lists: account codes, tax codes, customers, suppliers and so on. These lists should be concise and relevant to your business's transactions. As we work through the different Command Centres, we will explain how you can edit the lists to customise them for your business. At a bare minimum, an individual transaction involves a general ledger account code, a tax code, and a customer, a supplier or an employee. Grab a cup of tea and let's get started!

Day 1

Accounts Command Centre and Card File Centre

Key terms and concepts

▶ *General ledger account:* a collection of ledger accounts into which transactions are posted in total from journals. It holds the details of business transactions of the same type—that is, transactions related to particular types of asset, liability, income, owner's equity and expense items.

▶ *Chart of accounts:* a list of all the account names and numbers used in a business's general ledger, organised in such a way that it reflects the financial structure of the business. It serves as an index, enabling a given account to be located within the ledger.

▶ *Goods and services tax (GST):* a tax on goods and services sold within Australia. The tax (currently 10 per cent) is collected by the provider of the goods or service and remitted to the **Australian Taxation Office (ATO)** on a quarterly basis.

To start learning MYOB, your first step is to install MYOB software on your computer if it's not already there. You can download a free trial version of MYOB software from <www.MYOB.com.au>. To fully benefit from this book, I suggest you download MYOB AccountRight Plus if you use a PC or MYOB Account Edge if you use a Mac. Even if you have other MYOB software, you may like to do this for the purpose of working through this book. You will be able to create a data file that will last for 30 days, which is sufficient time to undertake all the exercises in this book.

Once you've installed MYOB AccountRight Plus, an MYOB AccountRight Plus icon will appear on your desktop (see figure 1.1).

Figure 1.1: MYOB AccountRight Plus desktop icon

Double-click the icon, and the MYOB welcome screen opens (see figure 1.2). This gives you access to the company data file.

We will start by creating a brand-new company file. The activities in this book are oriented around a small fitness studio called Green Apple Gym. Click 'Create a company file' on the left-hand side, and the New Company File Assistant: Introduction window opens (see figure 1.3). At this stage you can choose the MYOB product you wish to create: AccountRight Basics, AccountRight Standard or AccountRight Plus. Select AccountRight Plus.

Figure 1.2: MYOB welcome screen

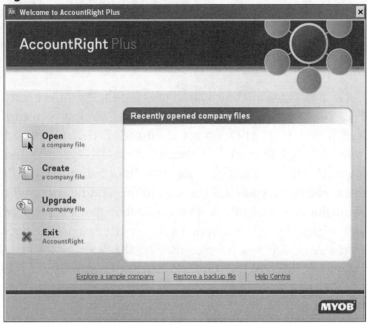

Figure 1.3: New Company File Assistant: Introduction

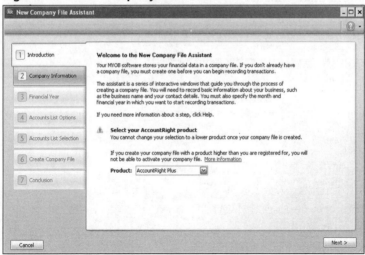

On the left-hand side of this screen you will see a **wizard** with seven tabs. The tab that is currently active is always violet. I encourage you to read the information on the MYOB screen, but I will specify the required options as we work through the wizard.

Click the Company Information tab, and the New Company File Assistant: Company Information window appears (see figure 1.4). The contact information that is entered here will feed through to other areas, such as reports and invoices. Fill out the fields with the information shown in this window. As you click through to the next field, the tabs along the left-hand side will become active. For the purpose of working through this book I suggest that you use the data I provide. Once you have completed the seven-day course you can go back to the start and enter your own data if you wish, as you are able to create an unlimited number of trial MYOB data files.

Figure 1.4: New Company File Assistant: Company Information window

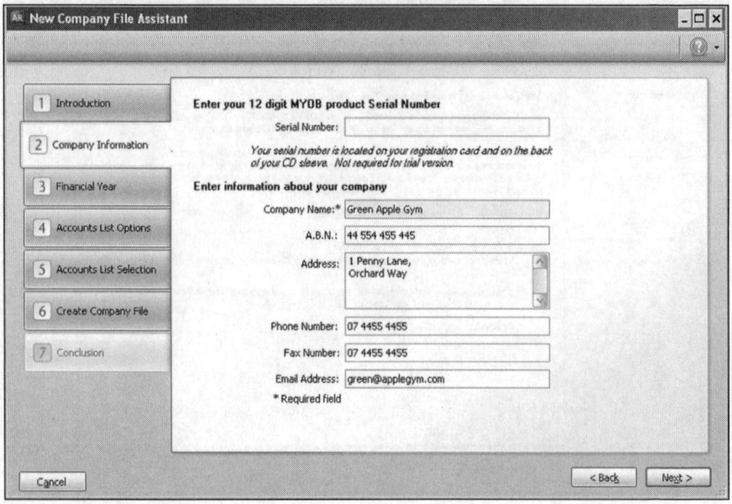

Click the Financial Year tab, and the New Company File Assistant: Financial Year window will open (see figure 1.5). This is where you enter the financial year you wish to start with. If you wish to enter data from a previous year, you will need to change the default financial year. If your business does not run along the standard 1 July to 30 June financial year, you can change the last month of the financial year here.

Before you move on, check that you have selected the correct financial year for your business, as you cannot change it later on. For the purpose of this exercise, accept the default fields that appear, which should reflect the current financial year.

Figure 1.5: New Company File Assistant: Financial Year window

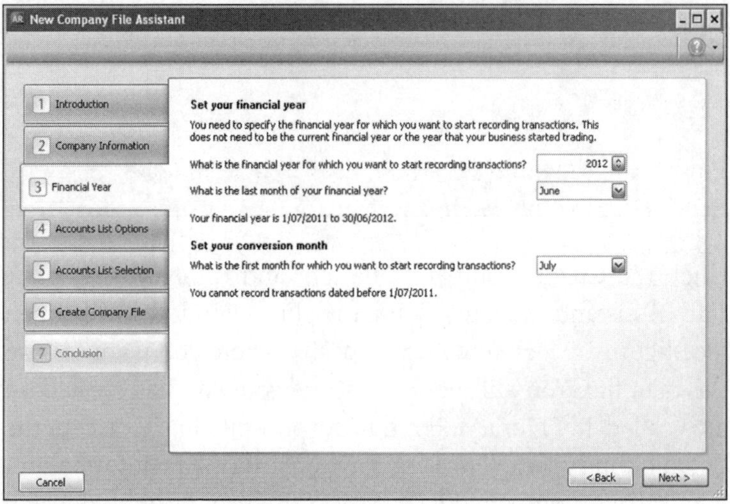

Click the Accounts List Options tab, and the New Company File Assistant: Accounts List Options window opens (see figure 1.6, overleaf). This area allows you to choose how you will set up the company's **chart of accounts**. As you can see, you have three choices. You can use the industry-specific list defined by MYOB; or you can import an accounts list; or, as we are going to do, you can select the third option, 'Build your own list'. Once you've selected the third option, the Accounts List Selection tab is deactivated and fades to grey.

Figure 1.6: New Company File Assistant: Accounts List Options window

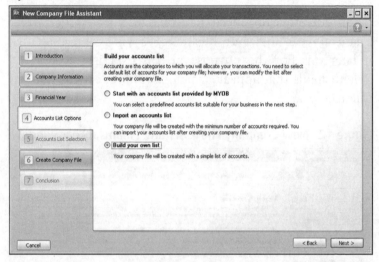

Click the Create Company File tab, and the New Company File Assistant: Create Company File window will open (see figure 1.7). Here you can specify where you want to save the data file. You will notice that the software has created an area called 'My Library'. For our purposes it's fine to accept the default library area. Once you have entered all the information, click Create Company File, and MYOB AccountRight Plus will take a few moments to create your new company file.

Once the new data file has been created, the New Company File Assistant: Conclusion window opens (see figure 1.8). Click the Command Centre button to access the company data file for the Green Apple Gym.

Figure 1.7: New Company File Assistant: Create Company File window

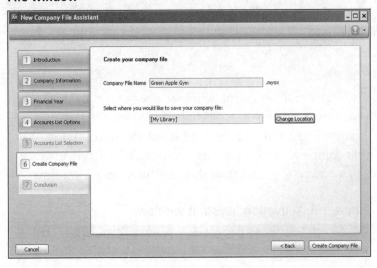

Figure 1.8: New Company File Assistant: Conclusion window

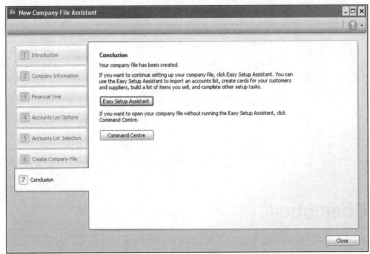

Note

If you close the data file before you have reached the end of this chapter, you will find instructions for opening the data file at the start of day 2.

The Activation Assistant window opens (see figure 1.9). It is at this window you would activate your purchased MYOB AccountRight software. Instead select the third option, 'I use this company file for practice, evaluation or study purposes.' Click Next and click OK at the next Information window.

Figure 1.9: Activation Assistant window

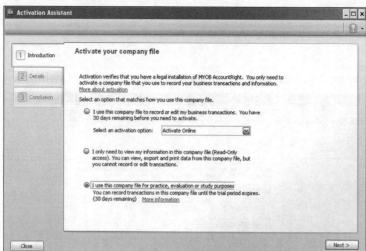

Orientation

Figure 1.10 shows the Accounts Command Centre home screen, which is essentially the MYOB home screen. While the basic elements are always as shown here, the specific information changes according to the Command Centre you have selected.

Figure 1.10: Accounts Command Centre home screen

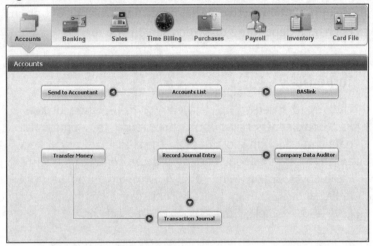

If you ever get lost within MYOB, click Esc (escape) on your keyboard—you may need to do this a few times—and you will return to this screen. If you are using a different version of MYOB, you may not be able to see all the icons across the screen. In this case click the maximise box in the top right-hand corner to make the screen full-size.

Menu bar

The menu bar at the top of the screen (see figure 1.11) looks and works very much like the menu bars in Microsoft software.

Figure 1.11: Command Centre menu bar

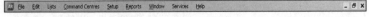

Most areas within MYOB AccountRight Plus can be accessed via the drop-down menus on the menu bar. Take some time to explore the different options available; most options are self-explanatory. Some may be greyed out, which means that those options are inactive at that point. The wording of options may change depending on which screen you are in.

Turbo Tip

The key to speeding up data entry is to use shortcut keys. Fast bookkeepers never touch the mouse; they process all data entry through shortcut keys. The available shortcut keys are shown on the menu bar's drop-down options. (The terms 'drop-down options' and 'drop-down menus' can be used interchangeably.) They typically consist of a combination of keys—for example, Ctrl + Y for Find Transactions.

Shortcut keys are one of three symbols you will see on the drop-down menus. These symbols are explained in table 1.1.

Table 1.1: symbols used on the MYOB menu bar's drop-down options

Symbol	Explanation
▶	An arrow pointing right directs you to further drop-down options.
...	Three dots (an ellipsis) indicate that a new window or dialogue box will open when you select this option.
—	An underscored letter indicates a short cut: press Alt (or Command on a Mac) followed by the underlined letter to execute the relevant command; e.g. F indicates that Alt + F will open the File drop-down menu.

You can download a full list of MYOB short cuts from <www.learnMYOBin7days.com>.

Drop-down options

The **File** drop-down options (see figure 1.12) enable you to manage the file as a whole. A new file can be created, and existing files can be opened, backed up or restored. The financial or payroll year can be closed off. You can print active documents and customised forms can be moved to a different location, using the Migrate Custom Forms option.

Figure 1.12: File drop-down options

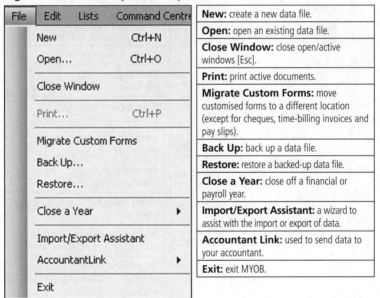

The **Edit** drop-down options (see figure 1.13, overleaf) allow you to format invoices and bills professionally via such options as Insert Line, Insert Header and Insert Subtotal. The typical editing tools, including Cut, Copy, Paste and Clear, are also available. If you are familiar with double-entry bookkeeping, you will like the Recap Transaction option, which allows you to review the double-entry bookkeeping journal created by the transaction.

Figure 1.13 Edit drop-down options

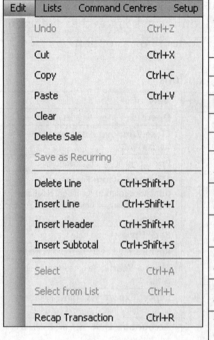

Edit	Lists	Command Centres	Setup
Undo		Ctrl+Z	
Cut		Ctrl+X	
Copy		Ctrl+C	
Paste		Ctrl+V	
Clear			
Delete Sale			
Save as Recurring			
Delete Line		Ctrl+Shift+D	
Insert Line		Ctrl+Shift+I	
Insert Header		Ctrl+Shift+R	
Insert Subtotal		Ctrl+Shift+S	
Select		Ctrl+A	
Select from List		Ctrl+L	
Recap Transaction		Ctrl+R	

Undo: in some cases this will allow you to undo one step within MYOB, but it doesn't work everywhere, so don't rely on it.

Cut: remove data to clipboard.

Copy: copy data to clipboard.

Paste: paste data from clipboard.

Clear: clear an area of data.

Delete Sale: erase data.

Save as Recurring: save a transaction as a recurring transaction.

Delete Line: delete a line within an invoice.

Insert Line: insert a line within an invoice.

Insert Header: insert a header within an invoice.

Insert Subtotal: insert a subtotal within an invoice.

Select: in an active area, this option will change to 'Select from relevant lists'.

Recap Transaction: review the double-entry bookkeeping entry created by the transaction.

The List drop-down options (see figure 1.14) provide access to all the different lists within MYOB. As MYOB is primarily built upon a database, it is critical that these lists have been compiled to be as efficient and meaningful as possible. In some cases this is the only area where the lists can be edited or deleted.

Figure 1.14: List drop-down options

Lists	Command Centres	Setup	Repor
Accounts			
Cards			
Activities			
Items			
Jobs			
Categories			
Tax Codes			
Recurring Transactions			
Payroll Categories			
Superannuation Funds			
Employment Classifications			
Custom Lists & Field Names			▶
Custom Lists			▶
Sales & Purchases Information			▶
Identifiers			

Accounts: general ledger accounts list.

Cards: Customer, Supplier, Employee and Personal Card files.

Activities: activities list.

Items: inventory items.

Jobs: job or project costings can be established here, but this option is beyond the scope of this book.

Categories: category lists that can be used across the balance sheet and profit and loss codes.

Tax Codes: list of tax codes used in the business.

Recurring Transactions: list of recurring transactions; recurring transactions can be deleted in this area.

Payroll Categories: list of payroll categories.

Superannuation Funds: list of employee superannuation funds and limited details of each fund.

Employment Classifications: list of employment classifications.

Custom Lists and Field Names: list of custom lists and field names.

Custom Lists: editable list of custom lists.

Sales and Purchase Information: list of sales and purchase information.

Identifiers: list of identifiers (e.g. N = newsletter).

Warehouse locations: only available in MYOB AccountRight Enterprise.

The Command Centres drop-down options (see figure 1.15, overleaf) offer a different way to access the eight different Command Centres within MYOB. The further options are identical to what is shown in the flowchart for each Command Centre and in the Command Panel area.

Figure 1.15: Command Centres drop-down options

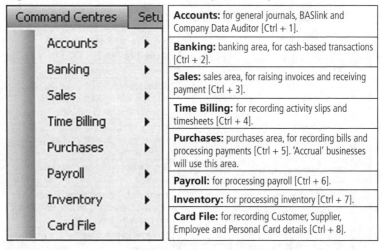

Command Centres	Setu	
Accounts	▶	**Accounts:** for general journals, BASlink and Company Data Auditor [Ctrl + 1].
Banking	▶	**Banking:** banking area, for cash-based transactions [Ctrl + 2].
Sales	▶	**Sales:** sales area, for raising invoices and receiving payment [Ctrl + 3].
Time Billing	▶	**Time Billing:** for recording activity slips and timesheets [Ctrl + 4].
Purchases	▶	**Purchases:** purchases area, for recording bills and processing payments [Ctrl + 5]. 'Accrual' businesses will use this area.
Payroll	▶	**Payroll:** for processing payroll [Ctrl + 6].
Inventory	▶	**Inventory:** for processing inventory [Ctrl + 7].
Card File	▶	**Card File:** for recording Customer, Supplier, Employee and Personal Card details [Ctrl + 8].

The Setup drop-down options (see figure 1.16) access the initial set-up options and preferences within the data file. These options allow you to customise forms, install payroll tax tables, and update company information.

Figure 1.16: Setup drop-down options

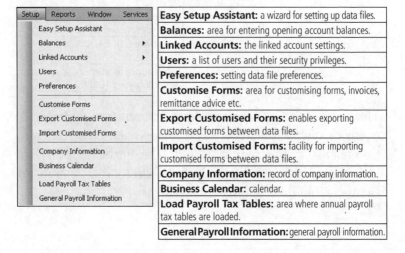

Setup Reports Window Services	
Easy Setup Assistant	**Easy Setup Assistant:** a wizard for setting up data files.
Balances ▶	**Balances:** area for entering opening account balances.
Linked Accounts ▶	**Linked Accounts:** the linked account settings.
Users	**Users:** a list of users and their security privileges.
Preferences	**Preferences:** setting data file preferences.
Customise Forms	**Customise Forms:** area for customising forms, invoices, remittance advice etc.
Export Customised Forms	**Export Customised Forms:** enables exporting customised forms between data files.
Import Customised Forms	**Import Customised Forms:** facility for importing customised forms between data files.
Company Information	**Company Information:** record of company information.
Business Calendar	**Business Calendar:** calendar.
Load Payroll Tax Tables	**Load Payroll Tax Tables:** area where annual payroll tax tables are loaded.
General Payroll Information	**General Payroll Information:** general payroll information.

The **Report** drop-down option (see figure 1.17) provides access to hundreds of customisable reports. With accurate, timely and complete transactional data entered, reports can provide a wealth of useful management information that can be used in the businesses decision-making process. If you are in a management position, I encourage you to spend time looking at reports. Delve into customisable reports and think about how you can use them to track performance and set goals for the business.

Figure 1.17: Reports drop-down options

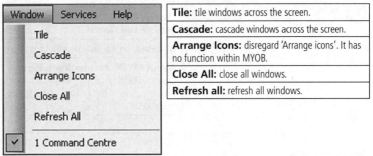

The **Window** drop-down options (see figure 1.18) allow you to manage the screens you are viewing to suit your processing needs. They also highlight which windows are currently active and provide a short cut to access them. This is especially useful when you are undertaking the bank **reconciliation**.

Figure 1.18: Window drop-down options

Tile: tile windows across the screen.	
Cascade: cascade windows across the screen.	
Arrange Icons: disregard 'Arrange icons'. It has no function within MYOB.	
Close All: close all windows.	
Refresh all: refresh all windows.	

Window menu items: Tile, Cascade, Arrange Icons, Close All, Refresh All, ✓ 1 Command Centre

The Services drop-down options (see figure 1.19, overleaf) provide direct access to additional online services from MYOB Australia.

Figure 1.19: Services drop-down options

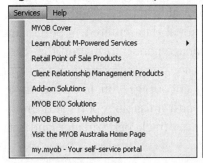

All of these options link to further information available on the MYOB Australia website.

The **Help** drop-down options (see figure 1.20) provide access to various forms of installed and online MYOB Help.

Figure 1.20: Help drop-down options

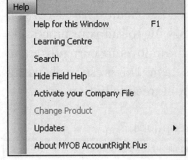

Help for this Window: customised help for the window currently open.

Learning Centre: link to the Help centre.

Search: search MYOB Help.

Hide Field Help: hovering over buttons will activate an explanatory pop-up box. You can turn this off in Preferences.

Activate your Company File: access to activating company file.

Change Product: change the AccountRight product you are using.

Updates: register and check for updates.

About MYOB AccountRight Plus: Opens a window displaying the name and version number of the software and copyright information.

Exercise 1.1

Take some time to familiarise yourself with the various features on the menu bar.

Command Centre and flowcharts

The next section down from the Menu Bar is called the Command Centre (see figure 1.21). This area gives you access to the different areas within MYOB, each represented by a coloured icon. When you click an icon, a flowchart showing the typical flow of work in that area appears. We will explore the various areas further on other days.

Figure 1.21: Command Centre icons

All the flowcharts have a similar structure. Those in the Banking, Sales, Purchases and Inventory Command Centres have a customised Register button at the top of the middle column and a Transaction Journal button at the bottom of the middle column. Note also that as you select different Command Centres some of the options on the menu bar and on the Command Panel will change accordingly. (We will explore some of these options later.) If you can't find what you need, stop and think: what am I trying to do, what does it relate to, what Command Centre would it fit within?

Accounts Command Centre

The Accounts Command Centre (see figure 1.22, overleaf) is home to a few really important functions within MYOB, although it is not an area you would visit every day. Typically you would come here weekly or monthly, depending on the number of transactions that are being processed. The Company Data Auditor is a useful tool that consolidates several end-of-period company file maintenance tasks in a single location, while the BASlink provides a template to assist with the preparation of **Business Activity Statements (BAS)**. The most important item here is the Accounts List—get this right and you have won half the battle.

Figure 1.22: Accounts Command Centre window

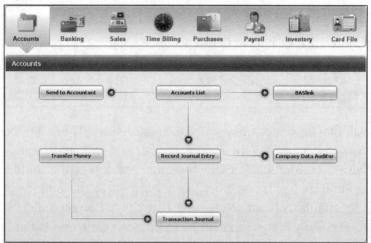

Banking Command Centre

The Banking Command Centre (see figure 1.23) is for the processing of day-to-day cash transactions: through Spend Money and Receive Money. Here you can prepare bank deposits, print receipts and issue remittance advices. (MYOB uses the plural noun 'advices', which although not strictly correct is commonly used in this context.) This is also where you perform the regular and important process of reconciling accounts. We will explore the Banking Command Centre further on day 2.

Figure 1.23: Banking Command Centre window

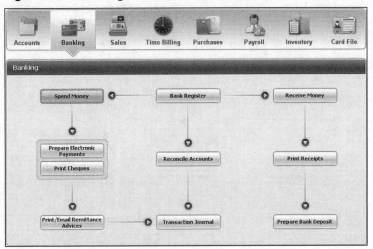

Sales Command Centre

Everything related to the sales department can be found in the Sales Command Centre (see figure 1.24, overleaf). Here you can produce and issue invoices and statements, analyse receivables and receive payment. We will explore the Sales Command Centre further on day 3.

Time Billing Command Centre

The Time Billing Command Centre (see figure 1.25, overleaf) is useful for tracking time spent with clients or on jobs. The data collected then flows through to detailed invoices and can be accounted for on employees' pay slips. Most MYOB users will not use this area, but it's very useful for businesses that charge by the hour. We will explore invoicing further on day 3, and payroll on day 6.

Figure 1.24: Sales Command Centre window

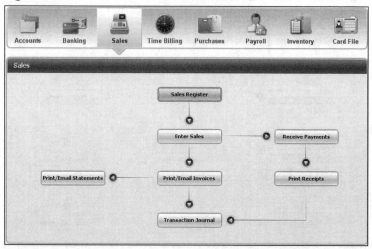

Figure 1.25: Time Billing Command Centre window

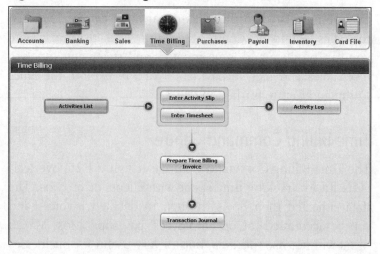

Purchases Command Centre

The Purchases Command Centre flowchart (see figure 1.26) almost mirrors the Sales Command Centre flowchart (see figure 1.24). This area is used for tracking purchases that are being processed on an **accrual accounting** basis. Purchases can be entered as a quote, an order or a bill, and payments owing can be monitored. We will explore the Purchases Command Centre further on day 4.

Figure 1.26: Purchases Command Centre window

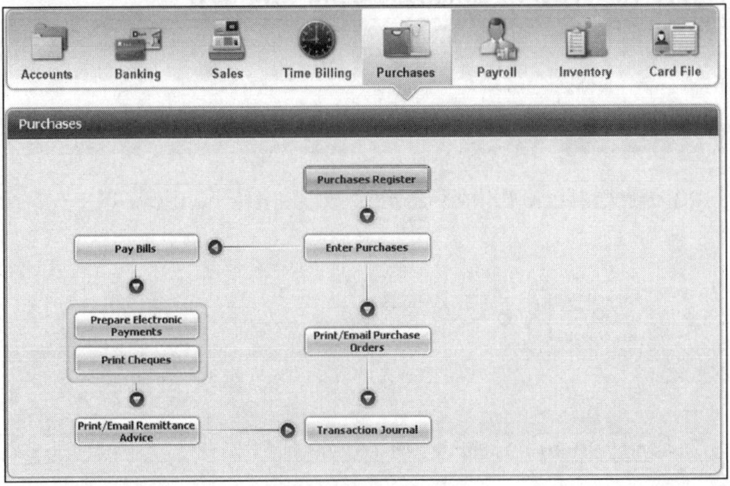

Payroll Command Centre

The Payroll Command Centre (see figure 1.27, overleaf) is a facility offered in AccountRight Plus and higher versions of MYOB software. This Command Centre covers all aspects of the payroll process. Employees can be added in the Card File area; activity slips and time sheets can be accessed from the Time Billing area; pay can be processed; payment summaries can be produced; superannuation and pay as you go (PAYG) withholding (which refers to the amount a business is obliged to withhold from the salary of its employees and remit to the ATO) can be paid; and the annual summary of payroll information known as the **EMPDUPE** files can be created. Using a computerised payroll system can be a major timesaver, especially during the busy period at the end of the payroll year. We will explore the Payroll Command Centre further on day 6.

Figure 1.27: Payroll Command Centre window

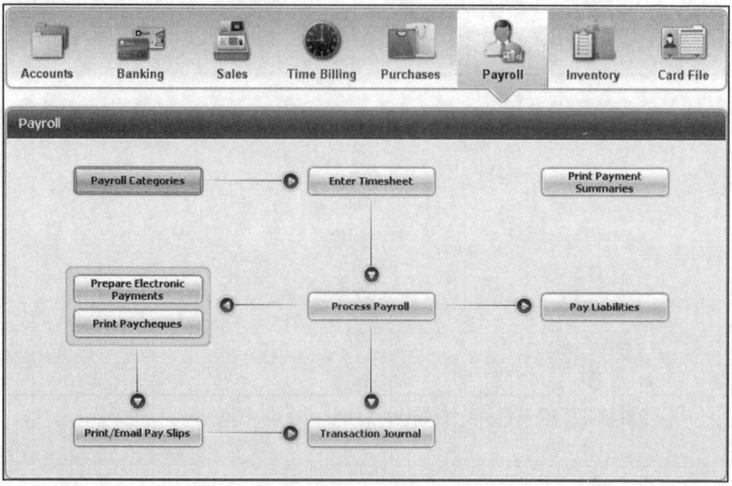

Inventory Command Centre

The Inventory Command Centre (see figure 1.28) gives you many useful options for recording and managing **inventory**. Individual inventory items can be set up on either a periodic or perpetual basis, and then purchased or sold, counted, or combined through an auto-build process. The auto-build process allows two or more items to be combined to create another item, typically for sale. We will explore the Inventory Command Centre further on day 5.

Figure 1.28: Inventory Command Centre window

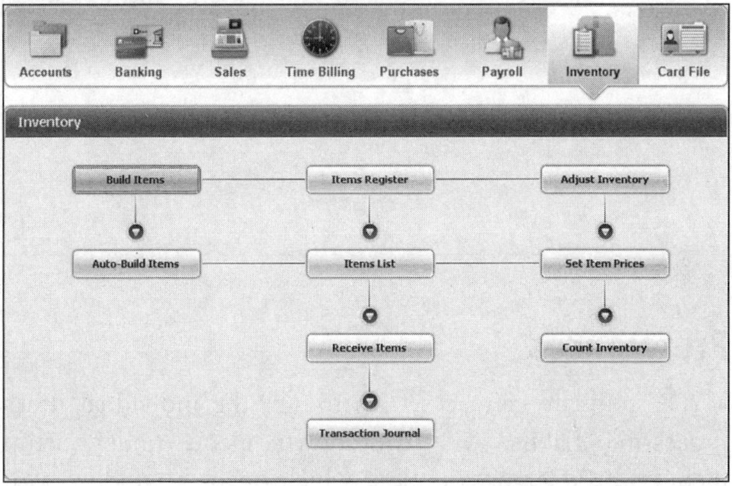

Card File Command Centre

The Card File Command Centre (see figure 1.29, overleaf) allows you to record the contact details of customers, suppliers, employees, and other parties referred to as 'personal'. Using three customer relationship manager tools—identifiers, custom lists and custom fields—you can easily adapt the information to suit the needs of your business. We will explore this Command Centre a little later today.

Figure 1.29: Card File Command Centre window

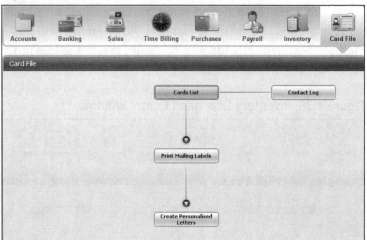

Preferences

MYOB software can be set up to suit the individual user's processing habits. The drop-down menu under Setup includes a Preferences option, which opens a window with the following tabs: System, Windows, Reports and Forms, Banking, Sales, Purchases, Inventory, and Security. Take a few moments to look at these different options; most are self-explanatory. In the case of MYOB multi-user software, if the notation '[System-Wide]' is at the end of the option, this means the preference will affect all users. Many preferences can be changed as you adapt to the software, although some cannot be switched off once they have been activated. In these cases a warning window will pop up to alert you to this fact.

System

The System tab accesses the rules that govern the behaviour of MYOB.

Windows

The Windows tab gives you access to the choices that change the look and feel of MYOB.

Reports and forms

The Reports and Forms tab allows you to specify the ageing period that applies to Receivables and Payables reports. Click the Email button at top left to access the editable field for all email messages generated by MYOB. You can overwrite the default messages within this field, but you need to be aware that you are confined to a predetermined number of characters.

Banking

The Banking tab gives you various options; for example, you can select how transactions will appear in the bank register.

Sales

The Sales tab allows you to access everything within MYOB that is related to sales. Note that you have the ability to change **credit** terms at the top left of the window (or at bottom right for older versions of the software).

Purchases

The Purchases tab provides options for dealing with quotes, orders and bills. For example, you can choose to be alerted if duplicate numbers are used or if the supplier does not have a recorded **Australian Business Number (ABN)** on file. This window is similar to the Sales Preference window, and has credit term settings at top left.

Inventory

The Inventory tab has just one setting, which allows you to use the standard cost as the default price on purchase orders and bills. (Earlier versions of MYOB had two settings.)

Security

The Security tab allows you to choose from a range of security options. A button at top left allows each user to set his or her individual password.

Exercise 1.2

Go to the Setup option on the menu bar and select Preferences. Select the Banking tab (see figure 1.30), and then check the boxes beside the following:

▶ Make a Contact Log Entry for Every Cheque

▶ Make a Contact Log Entry for Every Deposit

▶ Default Cheque is Already Printed

Uncheck all other boxes.

Figure 1.30: Preferences window: Banking tab

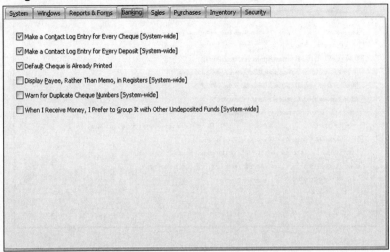

Select the Preferences window: Sales tab (see figure 1.31, overleaf). Check the following boxes:

▶ Warn if Customer has an Outstanding Credit Before Applying a Payment

▶ Make a Contact Log Entry for Every Sale

▶ Retain Original Invoice Number on Backorders

▶ Retain Original Invoice Number when Quotes Change to Orders or Invoices

▶ If Credit Limit is Exceeded on Sale [select Warn And Continue]

Uncheck all other boxes.

Figure 1.31: Preferences window: Sales tab

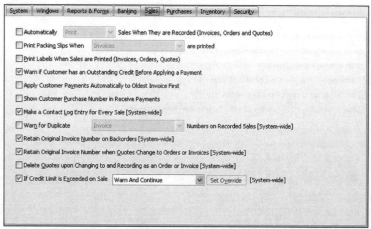

Select the Preferences window: Purchases tab (see figure 1.32). Check the following boxes:

▶ Warn if Supplier Owes Me Money Before Making a Supplier Payment

▶ Make a Contact Log Entry for Every Purchase

▶ Retain Original PO Number on Backorders

▶ Retain Original PO Number when Quotes Change to Orders or Bills

▶ Delete Quotes upon Changing to and Recording as an Order or Bill

▶ Warn if Supplier Does Not Have an ABN for Purchases Greater Than $75 Tax Exclusive

Uncheck all other boxes.

Figure 1.32: Preferences Window: Purchases tab

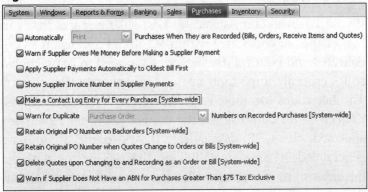

Select the Preferences window: Security tab (see figure 1.33). Check the following boxes:

▶ Prompt for Data Backup When Closing

▶ Check Company File for Errors before the Backup Process

Uncheck all other boxes.

Figure 1.33: Preferences window: Security tab

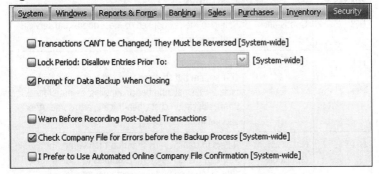

Once you have finished this exercise, click OK.

Tax codes

If your business is registered for **GST**, it is essential that you master the tax codes area within MYOB. MYOB records GST collected and paid via the tax codes allocated to transactions, so it's crucially important for these allocations to be correct. The tax codes are linked to the general ledger codes GST Collected and GST Paid. If the correct tax codes have been allocated, the GST automatically flows to the appropriate general ledger code. I would say that 95 per cent of the businesses I have worked with need only eight tax codes, but the most recent MYOB software starts with 10 tax codes, and if you are working with older MYOB software you may find that you have 15 or more tax codes. I find this confusing, and it can easily lead to errors, so the first thing I usually do is delete unnecessary tax codes. The most frequently used tax codes are listed in table 1.2.

Table 1.2: frequently used tax codes

Tax code	Name	Description
GST	Goods and services tax	Refers to the tax applied to most goods and services within Australia.
FRE	GST free	Applies to items that fall within the scope of the GST system but that are taxed at a rate of 0%. This includes a small number of supplies, essential food items, education costs, health care, and some other specific items.
N-T	Not reportable	Refers to transactions that don't fall within the scope of the GST system. Examples include wages, superannuation and intercompany transfers.

Tax code	Name	Description
ITS	Input taxed supply	Applies to income from financing activities, such as interest.
CAP	Capital acquisition tax	Applies to purchases that are deemed to be assets. Such purchases are listed under assets, not expenses. Your tax accountant will advise you of your business's threshold for deeming a purchase to be an asset. Typically such purchases are over $1000. This tax code is not allocated to the sale of a capital item.
GNR	Not registered for GST	Applies to purchases from a business that has an ABN but is not registered for GST.
NEG	GST on negative transactions	Used for the negative entry when a single transaction includes both income and expenses.
QUE	Query tax code	Used as a temporary code when you are processing a transaction and are unsure which tax code you should allocate. You would then investigate the matter further and allocate the correct code before processing the BAS.

If your business is not registered with the ATO for GST, all transactions entered will be deemed not reportable and assigned the N-T tax code in MYOB AccountRight. Even if you purchase items with GST on them, if you are not registered for GST you cannot claim back the GST.

Exploring a tax code

To fully understand tax codes, it's useful to see how they are set up. Go to the Lists option on the menu bar, select Tax Codes, and the Tax Code List window will appear. Double-click the GST row, and the Tax Code Information window appears (see figure 1.34, overleaf).

Figure 1.34: Tax Code Information window

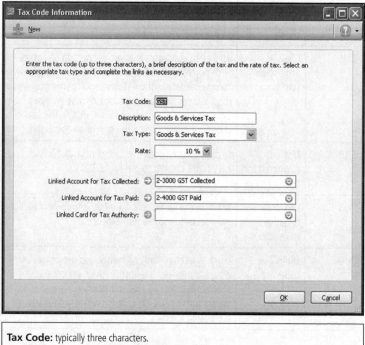

Tax Code: typically three characters.	
Description: a brief description of the tax.	
Tax Type: a description of the type of tax.	
Rate: changeable tax rate (GST is currently 10% but could change).	
Linked Account for Tax Collected: a liability clearing account called GST Collected.	
Linked Account for Tax Paid: a liability clearing account called GST Paid.	

GST Collected and GST Paid are both liability clearing accounts. We will discuss these concepts later today. Click OK and then Close.

Exercise 1.3

Creating a tax code

It's important to know how to create a tax code, as you may need a new code or one may be deleted accidentally. In this exercise we will create a Query Tax Code (QUE) as defined in table 1.2 (on p.30).

▶ Go to the Lists option on the menu bar and select Tax Codes.

▶ Go to the top left-hand corner (bottom left in older versions of MYOB) and click New to create a new tax code.

▶ In the Tax Code field, enter QUE, tab through to the Description field, and enter Query Tax Code.

▶ The tax type will be Goods and Services Tax. To be prudent, enter a 10 per cent tax code to ensure that you are not underestimating your tax obligation.

▶ The linked account for tax collected is GST Collected. Click in the drop-down box and enter '2-3000 GST Collected', then click tab.

▶ The linked account for tax paid is GST Paid. Click in the drop-down box and enter '2-4000 GST Paid', then click tab.

▶ Click OK, and a new tax code will be created.

Edit a tax code

It may be necessary to edit a tax code; for instance, if the government changed the GST rate, you would need to enter the new rate. In this example we are not going to change the GST rate; rather, you will learn a useful way of avoiding a common mistake. The code GNR means 'not registered for GST' (see table 1.2 on p. 30) but is frequently mistaken for the common GST tax code. Therefore, we will change the GNR tax code to read NRG.

▶ Go to the Lists option on the menu bar and select Tax Codes.

▶ Select the GNR Tax Code by hovering across the line and double-clicking it.

▶ In the Tax Code field, overwrite GNR with NRG.

Deleting a tax code

As mentioned earlier, I prefer to use a streamlined tax code list and therefore I delete all codes the business is unlikely to use. Here is how you would do this.

▶ Go to the Lists option on the menu bar and select Tax Codes.

▶ Select the ABN Tax Code by hovering across the line and double-clicking it.

▶ Right-click to bring up a context-sensitive shortcut menu, and select Delete Tax Code.

Exercise 1.4

Delete the following tax codes: INP, VWH and EXP.

Chart of accounts

The chart of accounts is a numerical list of **general ledger accounts** or account codes, and is the most important part of your accounting system. It is the backbone of the system, the structure upon which all transactions are based. It is critical to the success of your business that the chart of accounts be set up to meet the business's reporting requirements. The chart of accounts is split into eight separate areas in accordance with the general accounting rules: asset, liability, equity, income, cost of sales, expenses, other income, and other expenses.

To view the chart of accounts, click the Accounts Command Centre and then the Accounts List button. Take some time to look through the chart of accounts shown in this window (see figure 1.35). You will most likely be familiar with at least some of the terminology. The basic account categories are explained in table 1.3 (overleaf).

Figure 1.35: Accounts List window

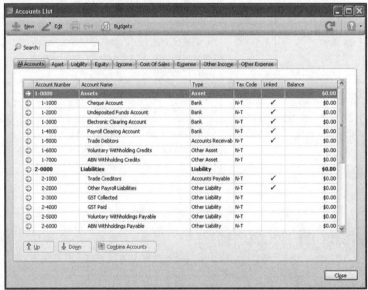

Table 1.3: basic account categories

Asset	1-XXXX	What the business owns; e.g. money in bank accounts (if the bank account is overdrawn, it will still remain in this area), cars, computers, buildings.
Liability	2-XXXX	What the business owes; e.g. credit card balances, bank loans.
Equity	3-XXXX	The net worth of the business — the part the owner(s) actually own (as opposed to the part funded by borrowings etc); e.g. current year earnings, retained earnings.
Income	4-XXXX	The money received from business activities, whether selling goods or providing services. Also referred to as revenue.
Cost of sales	5-XXXX	The cost of selling goods or services; e.g. if the business sold balls, this cost would include the purchase price plus freight. Also known as cost of goods sold.
Expenses	6-XXXX	General business expenses not directly related to the cost of providing the goods or services; e.g. telephone, rent.
Other income	7-XXXX	Income not related to the main purpose of the business; e.g. interest income.
Other expenses	8-XXXX	Expenses not directly related to the main purpose of the business; e.g. home office expenses, fines. (They may still be legitimate tax deductions.)

Turbo Tip

You will have noted the white arrows in the first column of the Accounts List window (see figure 1.33 on p. 29). This arrow, known as a zoom arrow or drill-down arrow, occurs in many different areas of MYOB. As the name suggests, it allows you to drill down to see further information. Once you have drilled down, you can simply click Esc to return to your starting point.

The second column of the Accounts List window lists the account numbers. The first digit of the account number represents the type of account; for example, 1 is assets and 4 is income. There are no universal account numbers; simply allocate numbers in a way that makes sense for your business. When you allocate numbers, it's a good idea to include enough digits to allow for future changes. For example, using 6-5010, 6-5011, 6-5012 and so on leaves you with no room to make changes, whereas using 6-5010, 6-5020, 6-5030 gives you plenty of scope to slot in additional account numbers if required. Numbering items consecutively allows you to group like items together; for example, you might number staff expenses 6-5010, 6-5020, 6-5030 and so on.

The third column is the account name. These names are editable, so use terms you can easily understand.

The fourth column is the account type, and the options vary accordingly. For example, the account type for Assets could be: Bank, Accounts Receivable, Other Current Asset, Fixed Asset or Other Asset. You can see that some of these options have been selected in figure 1.35 (on p. 35).

The fifth column shows the default tax code for the general ledger account.

The sixth column indicates whether the account is linked to other areas. MYOB software links relevant accounts, and this speeds up processing. Click the white zoom arrow beside 2-1000 Trade Creditors and then click the Details tab to see that this account has been linked to the Liability account for Tracking Payables.

The final column shows the current balance of the general ledger account.

Things to consider before reviewing accounts

Even though we selected the option of building our own chart of accounts, MYOB automatically provides us with many account lines that I think are unnecessary. But before you start reviewing the general ledger account lines and deciding on a chart of accounts for your own business, here are some issues you need to consider:

Measure what's important

Think about the type of information you find most useful when you are measuring your business performance and making decisions. If you sell products or services, can you clearly identify the income they generate? Likewise, can you identify the related cost of providing each product or service? By clearly defining this, you will be able to generate well-designed profit and loss statements that allow you to easily calculate the gross profit per product or per service. This, in turn, enables you to assess which products or services you should focus your energies on.

Use plain English

Use terms you can easily understand. If you always have to remind yourself what a particular term means, change it to something that's more meaningful to you to ensure that the profit and loss statement is easy to read and communicates the necessary information.

Summarise

Group like accounts together so that it's easy to subtotal them and therefore to generate higher-level reports giving information in summarised form. You can generate this level of report by selecting a Level 2 report in MYOB. This is the level that is most useful for management purposes, and is therefore the level I usually recommend to my MYOB clients. Just as you can drill up and down through Google Maps, your MYOB reports allow you to drill down from a high-level summary of the relevant information to several levels of detail below. For example, when you look at expenses in a Level 2 report, you see the primary groupings and the amounts rounded to whole dollars. If you need further information, you can drill down to the detail. This approach removes the 'noise' of many lines of information and gives the business owner a quick summary of the most relevant financial information.

Streamline

If MYOB AccountRight has generated account lines that you are unlikely to ever use, get rid of them. If you are splitting up expenses between landline telephone costs and mobile phone costs, for example, and it's not providing you with useful information, combine the accounts, remove the clutter and reduce the time you spend coding. There is no right or wrong number when it comes to the number of general ledger codes you should have, but as a general rule less is more.

Question how information is presented

Your accountant may generate your financial reports in alphabetical order, but that's unlikely to be useful to you. Don't be constrained by the alphabet; feel free to organise your reports in the way that is most meaningful to you—after all, that's what's most important to your business. You may be proactive and ask your accountant to return the financial statements in the same order that you generate them, but in reality not all accountants will comply with this request, or they may charge you for the privilege of getting the information returned to you in the same format you sent it to them.

Allow for growth

When creating new account lines, plan for growth at the outset. If your new range of health food bars really takes off, it may be more manageable to categorise them generically as 'Health food bar sales' than to try and identify each of them as a separate line item within the profit and loss statement. If it is important to know the sales of individual products, they can be tracked if they are set up as inventory items and all movement is associated with the defined inventory. Saying this, depending on the size of the company, I may still be inclined to list each motor vehicle (by license plate) individually as they are a significant investment for the business.

Exploring a general ledger account

Individual general ledger accounts will vary slightly depending on the types of transactions they record, but they all work in essentially the same way. To see how they work, let's take a look at a typical cheque account.

On the top left-hand side of figure 1.36 you will see two options: Header Account and Detail Account. The general ledger account can be either of these. Transactions can only be posted to detail accounts, so a banking account must be a detail account. Header accounts are used for grouping and subtotalling detail accounts, and on the MYOB screen they are always shown in bold.

Figure 1.36: Account Information window: Profile tab

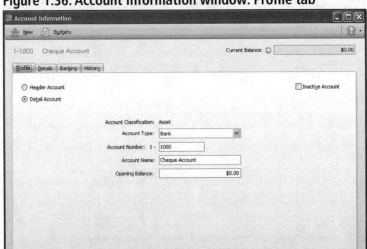

In the centre area are the details of this account code: the number, the name and the opening balance. I recommend that you don't enter an opening balance here and instead do it through a journal entry, as this is an editable area and any changes made here, whether deliberately or accidentally, can lead to future errors.

The Account Information Window: Details tab (see figure 1.37, overleaf) provides an area where you can describe the general ledger account code and allocate the typical default tax code. In the description area you can, if you wish, include typical transactions that would be posted to this account. Linked accounts are shown towards the bottom of the screen—in this example, Customer Receipts, Paying Bills and Cheque Payments.

Figure 1.37: Account Information window: Details tab

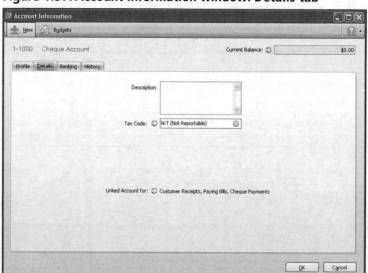

Only bank accounts have the Banking tab, shown in figure 1.38. In this window, there are fields to enter the bank account details and details related to electronic banking. These fields are activated when the 'I Create Bank Files' option is ticked.

Figure 1.38: Account Information window: Banking tab

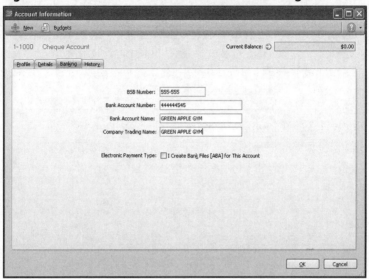

Exercise 1.5

Enter the banking details as they appear in figure 1.38: Account Information window: Banking tab.

The final tab in the Account Information window is the History tab (see figure 1.39, overleaf). This shows the month-by-month transactions in the account for the current and previous financial year. The current balance is shown at top right, and the zoom arrow enables you to drill down for detailed information about transactions posted against this code.

Figure 1.39: Account Information window: History tab

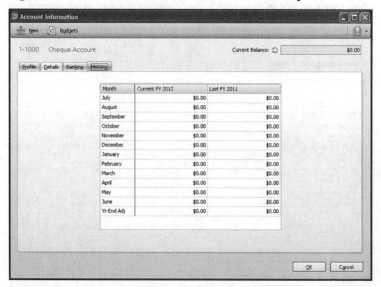

Exercise 1.6

Creating a new general ledger account

Owners of **small businesses** frequently pay for business items out of their own personal cash, and this, too, is a transaction that needs to be recorded within MYOB AccountRight. I recommend micro business clients rather than handling petty cash. It is good to set up a loan account in liabilities to allocate any accidental personal expenditure through the business or expenditure on the business. This reduces the hassle of dealing with petty cash and enables you to easily allocate a personal portion of a business expense. I typically reconcile my own personal loan account quarterly; I calculate what money I have withdrawn from the business and process that as a wage to myself, reducing the loan account to zero. In this exercise we will set up a loan account for this purpose, as shown in figure 1.40.

Figure 1.40: Account Information window: Profile tab: 2-9000 Loan—Owner's Name

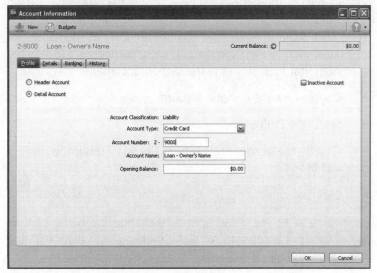

▶ Go to the Accounts Command Centre and click the Accounts List button.

▶ Go to the top left-hand side (bottom left in older versions of MYOB) and click New to create an account.

▶ Select Detail Account.

▶ Select the Account Type as Credit Card.

▶ Select the Account Number as 2-9. (The 000 will fill out automatically.)

▶ Enter as the Account Name: Loan – Owner's Name.

▶ Leave the Opening Balance as zero.

▶ Click OK, then click Close.

Editing an account

If the names of the general ledger accounts that appear in MYOB AccountRight are unfamiliar to you, you can edit them. I suggest to my clients that they use the account numbers as the names for their bank or credit card accounts, as these numbers are usually the references that appear on the transaction document.

► Double-click the Cheque account.

► Select the Profile tab.

► Change the Account Name from Cheque Account to ANZ 44444454.

► Click OK.

I also suggest to my clients that they change the name of their payroll liabilities account to PAYG Withholding, as it aligns with the ATO's terminology.

► Double-click 2-2000, Other Payroll Liability.

► Select the Profile tab.

► Change the Account Number to 2-2100.

► Change the Account Name to PAYG Withholding.

► Click OK.

A small business would usually have at least two payroll liabilities; superannuation liability and PAYG Withholding. For management and reporting purposes, it's advisable to group them together in a header account called Payroll Liability, as shown in figure 1.41. The two Detail sub-accounts will be indented and sit underneath it. Because they were created under a Header account they indent automatically, but if it's necessary to indent them, select the account and click the Down button at the bottom of the window (see figure 1.35 on p. 35).

Figure 1.41: Account Information window: Profile tab: 2-2000 Payroll Liability

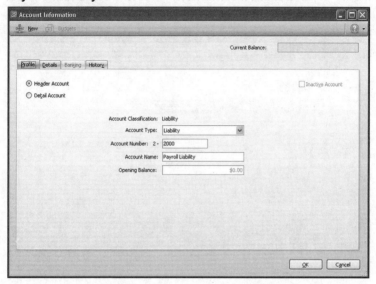

► Go to the Accounts Command Centre and click the Accounts List button.

► Go to the top left-hand side and click New to create an account.

► Select Header account.

► Select the Account Type: Liability.

► Select the Account Number: 2-2.

► Enter the Account Name: Payroll Liability.

▶ Click the Details tab (see figure 1.42) and check the box 'When Reporting, Generate a Subtotal for This Section'.

▶ Click OK.

Figure 1.42: Account Information window: Details tab: 2-2000 Payroll Liability

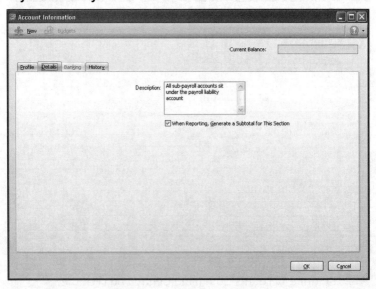

When payroll is processed, superannuation accrues in the Superannuation Liabilities account until it is paid into the employees' superannuation fund(s). This is a Detail account that will sit under the Payroll Liability Header account.

▶ Click New to create an account.

▶ Select Detail account.

▶ Select the Account Type: Other Liabilities.

▶ Select the Account Number: 2-22.

▶ Enter the Account Name: Superannuation Liabilities.

▶ Click OK.

Clearing accounts

A clearing account is a bookkeeping mechanism for managing the movement of transactions within the accounts.

Some clearing accounts are obvious from their name, such as Electronic Clearing account and Payroll Clearing account, but others, such as Trade Creditors, Trade Debtors, GST Collected, GST Paid, and **PAYG Withholding**, are not so obvious. These you need to learn to recognise.

To help you understand the purpose of a clearing account, let's examine the liability account PAYG Withholding.

As payroll is processed, PAYG is withheld from employees' pay and transferred to the PAYG Withholding liability account. The PAYG gradually accumulates in this account. When PAYG is paid to the ATO, the balance of the PAYG Withholding liability account clears to zero. (Think of the clearing account as a bucket that fills and then empties.) Every time a PAYG payment is made to the ATO, you need to reconcile the PAYG Withholding liability account to a zero balance.

If the balance of this account is not zero, the current balance should relate to recent explainable transactions.

In summary, clearing accounts act as temporary holding accounts for accrued money, and their balance should be explainable and regularly cleared to zero.

Card File Command Centre

One of my favourite areas in MYOB is the Card File Command Centre, because it acts as a simple customer resource management (CRM) tool. Full contact details of customers, suppliers, employees and other parties referred to as 'personal' can be stored here, along with other customised information.

Setting up a typical Customer Card

Go to the Card File Command Centre and click Card List, then click the New button at the top right-hand corner (or bottom right for older versions of MYOB) and enter The Fit Shoppe in the Name field.

Across the top of the Customer Card you will see six tabs: Profile, Card Details, Selling Details, Payment Details, Contact Log, Jobs and History (see figure 1.43).

Figure 1.43: Customer Card window: Profile tab

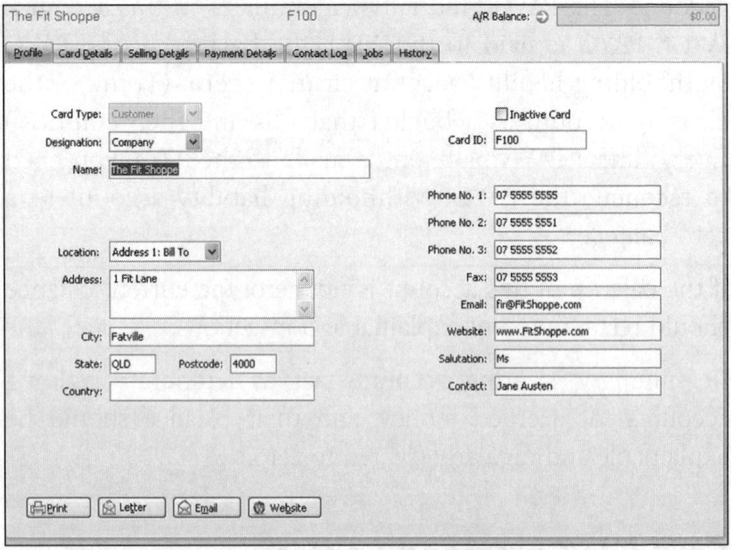

The Profile tab stores basic contact information, such as address, phone numbers, website and email details. Fill out the data as shown in figure 1.43, and then click the Card Details tab.

The Card Details tab allows you to store an image and brief notes (see figure 1.44). The image remains outside the MYOB database and so does not increase the size of your file. Various items of information are captured through the Identifiers, Custom Lists and Custom Fields. (These are explained below.) This is a simple but useful CRM tool and includes a mail merge feature, yet I find it is underutilised by many MYOB users who are not using another CRM tool. Utilising these fields will allow you to capture more information about your clients, which in turn can be used to generate reports that help you to make informed business decisions.

Figure 1.44: Customer Card window: Card Details tab

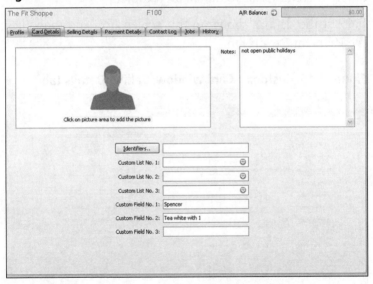

Identifiers are one-letter labels that can be assigned to cards. For example, it's common to use the letter N for newsletter and to assign an N identifier to the cards of all customers who wish to receive a newsletter. A report can then be generated listing the address details of these customers.

Custom Lists allows you to generate three separate defining lists of data. You can then select these lists to generate reports for management decision-making purposes. For example, Custom List 1 could be renamed Age Group, and the associated list could include Baby Boomers, Gen Y and Gen X.

Custom Fields allow you to enter a single piece of information in a field, such as the name of your contact's assistant.

Fill out the data as shown in figure 1.44 (on p. 51), and then click the Selling Details tab.

The Customer Card: Selling Details tab (see figure 1.45) allows you to customise sales invoices. For example, you can offer different credit terms to different customers.

Fill out the data as shown in this screenshot, and then click the Payment Details tab.

Figure 1.45: Customer Card window: Selling Details tab

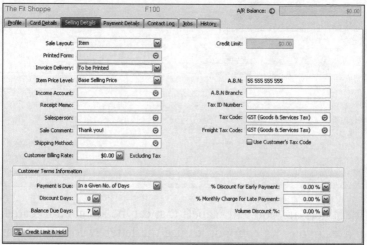

The Customer Card: Payment Details tab (see figure 1.46) allows you to record details of the customer's usual method of payment.

Figure 1.46: Customer Card window: Payment Details tab

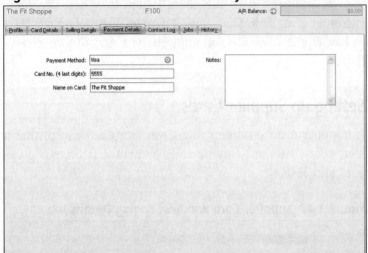

Fill out the data as shown in this screenshot, and then click the Contact Log tab.

The Contact Log is an area where you can record brief details of communications with the customer concerned. It also allows you to set up reminders for the To Do List on the Command Panel, which we will explore on day 7. This can be very useful, especially when debt collecting, as you can record your debt-collecting efforts and refer back to the customer's history.

The Jobs tab provides an overview of incomplete and completed jobs linked to the card file. Jobs refers to the costings of a project undertaken by the business, but this topic is beyond the scope of this book.

The History tab provides a month-by-month summary of transactions for 24 months, as well as other statistics about your relationship with the client: when they first became a customer, Last Sale Date, Last Payment Date, Average Days to Pay, Highest Invoice Amount, Highest Account Receivable Balance.

Setting up Supplier Cards

A Supplier Card is similar to a Customer Card except that it stores the customer's buying and payment details (see figures 1.47 and 1.48).

Figure 1.47: Supplier Card window: Buying Details tab

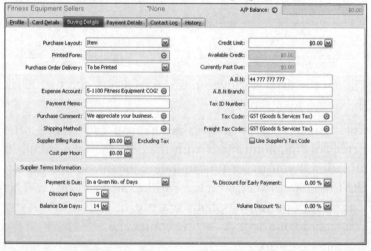

As shown in figure 1.48, the payment details automatically appear in capital letters when entered in the Payment Details tab. This information is required if electronic payments are processed via MYOB.

Figure 1.48: Supplier Card window: Payment Details tab

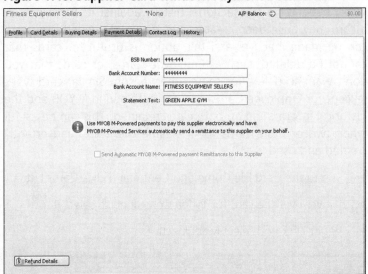

Exercise 1.7

▶ Go to the Card File Command Centre and click Cards List.

▶ Go to the top left-hand side and click New to create a new card.

▶ Create a new card for Fitness Equipment Sellers; make sure you select the Supplier Card Type field at the top.

▶ Enter the information from figures 1.47 and 1.48. Click OK.

▶ Create a Customer Card for Tonga Consulting.

Deleting or combining cards, or marking them as inactive

A card can be deleted, which means that it is completely removed from the MYOB system, or it can be marked inactive, which means that it will not show up on the selection list. Cards can also be combined, meaning that all transactions are moved to the primary card.

A card (except for an Employee Card) can be deleted in MYOB when there is no transactional history against it. For example, a card may have been created and then not needed. Any card can be made inactive, and this option is useful for cards that cannot be deleted, such as Employee Cards, or cards that you don't want to delete for some other reason. Similar card types (except for Employee Cards) can be combined in MYOB and the historical information on both cards retained. This can be useful when two or more cards for the same client are inadvertently created and used.

▶ Go to the Card File Command Centre and click Cards List.

▶ Hover over the card for Tonga Consulting to select it.

▶ Right-click and select Mark Inactive.

Exiting MYOB

Wow! What a huge day. You will be pleased to hear it is now time to exit MYOB. Go to the menu bar and click File, and then click Exit on the drop-down menu. Click Yes at the next screen, and then click Backup. Now your MYOB AccountRight data file is backed up and closed.

Summary of day 1

Today has been your introduction to MYOB business management software. You may have found some of the accounting terminology different to what you have learnt in the past. I agree, it took me a while to get my head around some of the terminology used in MYOB AccountRight software. As we work through the book, for simplicity, I will adhere to the MYOB AccountRight terminology.

Today we set up a data file from scratch and discussed some of the fundamentals of accounting and bookkeeping that will enhance your ability to correctly use MYOB AccountRight. We looked at the Menu Bar and the many drop-down options available to us. You should now feel familiar with the Command Centres, the Chart of Accounts and the Card File Command Centres, and with some other specific areas such as tax codes. Remember there is always a number of different ways to work in MYOB AccountRight. Stop and think about what you are trying to do, and move to the correct command panel. This should ensure the correct buttons are easily accessible.

It goes without saying that the initial set-up of the MYOB AccountRight data file is extremely important to the ongoing successful use of your software. As you start to use it, if you find there are aspects you don't like, remember you may have alternative set-up preferences available to you.

Take some time to review what we have covered today. We will build on this knowledge in day 2 when we will explore the Banking Command Centre.

Day 2

Banking Command Centre

Key terms and concepts

▶ *Cash accounting:* an accounting system where income and expenditure are recognised when the cash is received or paid.

▶ *Accrual accounting:* an accounting system where transactions and other events are recognised when they occur, not as cash is gained or paid.

▶ *Reconciliation:* the process of comparing financial statements such as bank accounts with the relevant ledger to ensure that they are in agreement.

Introduction and overview

Welcome to day 2. Today we are going to look at the Banking Command Centre, building on what you learned on day 1. As the first step, you need to open up the data file. Double-click the MYOB AccountRight icon on your desktop, and the MYOB welcome screen should appear. This will look the same as the window shown in figure 1.2 on page 3 (on day 1) except that under the heading Recently Opened Company Files you should see Green Apple Gym.myox. Select Green Apple Gym. myox and click the Open File button. The sign-on window should appear. Click OK and the Activation Assistant window will open. Select the third option, 'I use this company file for practice, evaluation or study purposes'. Click next and click OK at the Next Information window and finally you should now be in familiar territory.

If you are using an older version of MYOB software, double-click the MYOB AccountRight icon on your desktop and the welcome screen will appear. Click Open and the area will open up to where the backed-up file is. You then need to click the 'Look in' field and drop back one directory level (that is, click the folder one level above), and then double-click Green Apple Gym.myo to open the file you created on day 1.

The Banking Command Centre flowchart (see figure 2.1) is an area you will visit regularly to process incomings and outgoings of cash, review transactions in the register, and undertake regular reconciliations. Some straightforward businesses that use **cash accounting** and do not offer credit can operate solely in this area if they so choose.

Figure 2.1: Banking Command Centre flowchart

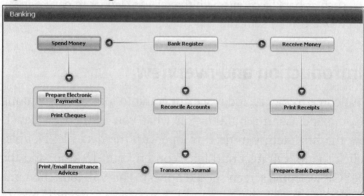

Before we explore what can be done in the Banking Command Centre, we need to look at the accounting methods that are appropriate for different types of businesses and the underlying linked accounts.

Cash versus accrual-based accounting

Business records can be processed on either a cash or accruals (non-cash) basis. In a cash accounting system transactions are recognised (that is, accounted for) when the cash is received or paid. In an accrual-based accounting system transactions and other events are recognised when they occur, not as cash is gained or paid. Accrual-based accounting provides a fairer representation of business activities because transactions are reported in the period they reflect rather than in the period in which they are incurred. Cash accounting is easier and quicker to process. For example, in accrual-based accounting the expense of annual insurance would be divided by 12 and recognised in every applicable month, whereas in cash-based accounting the expense would be recognised only when it was paid.

In Australia, small businesses as defined by the ATO—those with an annual turnover of less than $2 million—typically opt to report GST on a cash accounting basis. Their business tax records may well be processed on an accruals basis, but on a day-to-day basis their transactions and Activity Statements (BAS and IAS, which we will cover on day 7) are processed on a cash basis.

If you are unsure which accounting basis a business uses for GST purposes, check with the accountant or at the top right-hand corner of the ATO-issued Business Activity Statement.

Cash versus accrual in relation to MYOB

If your business uses accrual-based accounting, any transactions that did not occur on the day they were paid for will need to be processed via the Sales Command Centre and Purchases Command Centre in order to ensure that they are recorded and reported in the appropriate period. Most reports generated within MYOB are prepared on an accruals basis, and are exclusive of GST.

If, however, your business works on a cash basis (like most small businesses in Australia), you can process transactions in the Banking, Sales or Purchases Command Centres. While it is faster to process transactions in the Banking Command Centre via Spend Money/Receive Money, because this is a one-step process, it retains less information. When you use the Sales or Purchases Command Centres, you can enter more details, the transaction will appear on Sales or Purchases reports, and you have the ability to record different invoice and transaction dates. We will explore the Sales and Purchases Command Centres further on day 3 and day 4 respectively.

In MYOB, you can view a profit and loss report prepared on a cash basis by looking under Accounts and then under the subheading Small Business Entity. There is only one cash profit and loss report, as all the other profit and loss reports in MYOB will have been prepared on an accruals basis.

Linked accounts

As we discussed on day 1, MYOB allows you to link appropriate accounts with one another, which makes it faster to process transactions. For example, the Accounts and Banking Linked Accounts window (see figure 2.2) shows the five linked accounts that relate to the Banking Command Centre. This can be found under Setup → Linked Accounts → Accounts and Banking Accounts.

Figure 2.2: Accounts and Banking Linked Accounts window

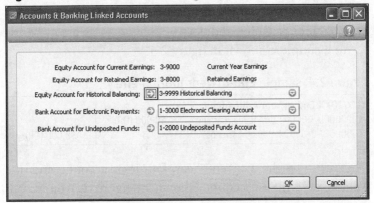

Current Year Earnings (see figures 2.2 and 2.3) are accrued earnings for the current year. This account is found under 'equity' on the balance sheet, and is taken from the net profit or loss calculated in the current profit and loss (accrual) report. Think about that — the final net profit or loss figure is entered on the balance sheet. Check this in your own reports. The balance sheet reflects the basic accounting equation (assets – liabilities = equity). Equity consists of the capital the owner contributed to the business plus retained earnings plus the current year's earnings.

Figure 2.3: Chart of Accounts window: Equity tab

Account Number	Account Name	Type	Tax Code	Linked	Balance
3-0000	Equity	Equity			$0.00
3-1000	Owner's Equity	Equity	N-T		$0.00
3-8000	Retained Earnings	Equity	N-T	✓	$0.00
3-9000	Current Year Earnings	Equity	N-T	✓	$0.00
3-9999	Historical Balancing	Equity	N-T	✓	$0.00

Retained Earnings are earnings brought forward from previous financial years. When the financial year is closed off and the data file is rolled over to the following financial year, an end-of-year journal entry is created to close off Current Year Earnings and transfer the balance to Retained Earnings. This entry cannot be edited and does not have a zoom arrow beside it. An example is shown in figure 2.4.

Figure 2.4: sample end-of-year journal entry

1/7/20XX End of Year Adjustment	
GJ000000 3-9000 Current Year Earnings $8,000 (DR)	
GJ000000 3-8000 Retained Earnings	$8,000 (CR)

The links to the Current Year Earnings account and the Retained Earnings account (shown in figure 2.3 on p. 63) cannot be changed.

The Historical Balancing account should always be zero, and if it isn't you need to investigate this and resolve the underlying problem. Accounting is based on the basic principles of double-entry bookkeeping, and a non-zero balance indicates that these principles have not been adhered to. Typically this happens either when amounts have been directly posted to the Historical Balancing account or when the opening entries have not been entered via a general journal.

Look back at the Accounts and Banking Linked Accounts window (see figure 2.2 on p. 63). The Electronic Clearing account should have either a zero or an explainable balance. (You will recall that we discussed clearing accounts on day 1.) In MYOB you can select payments and nominate that they be processed via electronic banking. A file is then created and needs to be manually uploaded to the business's bank. Because of this, all transactions sitting in the clearing account should be recent. If any are not recent, you need to look into the reasons for this.

Similarly, the Undeposited Funds account should have either a zero or an explainable balance. This account aids in the reconciliation process and is useful for businesses that process the receipt of money and then do their banking at the end of the day.

The links to Historical Balancing, Electronic Clearing and Undeposited Funds can be changed, but I strongly recommend that you don't do this. If you are using an existing data file and they are different from what is shown here, you would be wise to investigate why this is so.

Now that we have explored the linked accounts and the accounting basis used within the business, take some time to review the various options found on the Banking Command Centre flowchart and then put what you have learned into practice by completing the following exercises.

Exercise 2.1

Create the following general ledger accounts as seen in table 2.1.

Table 2.1: general ledger accounts

Account number	Account name	Type	Tax code
4-1100	Fitness Equipment	Income	GST
4-1210	Fitness Accessories	Income	GST
4-2100	1 on 1 Fitness Class Income	Income	GST
4-2200	Group Training Income	Income	GST
5-1100	Fitness Equipment COGS	COS	GST
5-1210	Fitness Accessories COGS	COS	GST
5-9200	Discount for Early Payments	COS	GST
6-1100	Office Stationery	Expense	GST

Table 2.1: *(cont'd)*

Account number	Account name	Type	Tax code
6-1110	Bank Charges	Expense	FRE
6-1200	Telephone Expenses	Expense	GST
6-1150	Postage	Expense	GST
6-5300	Uniforms	Expense	GST
6-7100	Rent	Expense	GST
6-7200	Cleaning Expenses	Expense	GST
3-1000	Owner's Equity	Equity	N.T

Delete the following general ledger accounts (see table 2.2). Open the general ledger account → Edit → Delete Account.

Table 2.2: general ledger accounts

1-6000	Voluntary Withholding Credits	Asset
2-5000	Voluntary Withholding Payables	Liability

Create the following new cards (see table 2.3). Enter an ABN and any additional profile or card details data you wish.

Table 2.3: card data

Card Type	Name	Address	Expense/ income account	Sale/ purchase layout
Customer	Tonga Consulting			Professional
Customer	ABC Pty Ltd	1 Sandy Lane, Beach Nook	4-1100 Fitness Equipment Sales	
Supplier	Office Stationery Supplier	1 King Street	6-1100 Office Stationery	
Supplier	EDP Advisers			
Supplier	Andy's Rental Agency	1 Griffith Lane	6-7100 Rent	

Card Type	Name	Address	Expense/ income account	Sale/ purchase layout
Supplier	Australia Post		6-1150 Postage	
Supplier	Telstra		6-1200 Telephone Expenses	
Supplier	Wicking Uniforms		6-5300 Uniforms	
Supplier	Panda Cleaning Services			Professional
Employee	Rosemary Bostick			

Bank Register and Transaction Journal

The Bank Register and the Transaction Journal are found in the middle column of the Banking Command Centre flowchart (see figure 2.1 on p. 60). Both of these options can be accessed in the Banking, Sales, Purchases and Inventory Command Centres. The Bank Register (see figure 2.5) and the Transaction Journal (see figure 2.7 on p. 69) are similar in that all transactions can be found within them and they are sorted by date. You can view details of the transaction, including those linked to a specific bank account or credit card account, by clicking on the zoom arrow or double-clicking the entry.

Figure 2.5: Banking Command Centre: Bank Register window

	Date	Src	ID No.	Payee	Account	Withdrawal	Deposit	Balance
	1/10/2011	CR	CR000003	Owner cash injection	3-1000		$30,000.00	$30,000.00
	14/10/2011	CD	10	Marcia Brown Pay		$861.60		$29,138.40
	14/10/2011	CD	8	Rosemary Bostick Pay		$1,650.00		$27,488.40
	14/10/2011	CD	9	Tania Jones Pay		$2,328.00		$25,160.40
	31/10/2011	CD	BS	Monthly Bank Charges	6-1110	$5.00		$25,155.40
	1/11/2011	CD	EFT	Fortnightly Rent	6-7100	$500.00		$24,655.40

(Figures 2.5, 2.6 and 2.7 are examples only; there will be no transactions in your data file.) In figure 2.5 you will see columns for Withdrawal, Deposit and Balance; the Balance column calculates the running balance automatically. The latest version of MYOB allows for the Bank Statement to be imported via the Bank Register, whereas previously this could only be done during the reconciliation process. The columns can be interchanged, which is useful when you are comparing the Bank Register to the bank statement

Turbo Tip

The Data Entry Panel (see figure 2.6) is a short cut for entering different types of transactions (for example, Spend Money). You will find this at the bottom of the Bank Register screen.

Figure 2.6: Banking Command Centre: Bank Register Data Entry Panel

The Transaction Journal (see figure 2.7) groups entries in terms of the type of transaction processed: General Journal (GJ), Disbursements Journal (CD), Cash Receipts (CR), Sales Journal (SJ), Purchases Journal (PJ), and Inventory Journal (IJ). The two-letter reference identifies the source, is attached to the transaction and can be seen when you click the All tab. Within the relevant journal the transaction is split into its various parts: date, accounts to which amounts are to be posted, amounts to be posted to each account, and whether these amounts are a **debit** or a credit. There is also a space for a brief memo recording sources and other relevant details. This is shown in figure 2.7. The debit and credit side of the journal entry must always tally.

Figure 2.7: Banking Command Centre: Transaction Journal

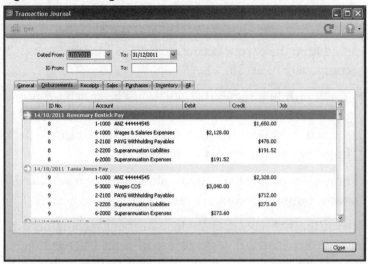

If you have learned double-entry bookkeeping, you will find this area reassuring. If you haven't, you might find it somewhat confusing. It is not the purpose of this book to explain double-entry bookkeeping, but it may be helpful if we take a look at a typical journal entry, as shown in figure 2.8.

Figure 2.8: a typical journal entry

5/11/20XX Office Stationery Supplies-OCT		
1-1000 Cheque Account		$70 (CR)
6-1100 Office Stationery	$63.64(DR)	
2-4000 GST Paid	$6.36 (DR)	

▶ The first line is the date and the memo. For audit trail purposes it is advisable to take the time to include a brief memo or at least to note the reason for the transaction.

▶ The second line shows that $70 has been credited from the cheque account. (This means that $70 has left the cheque account, so the balance has decreased.)

▶ The third line shows that $63.64 has been debited to the Office Stationery account. Note that office stationery expenses have increased by $63.64, not $70 (the amount paid from the cheque account), as the $70 included a GST component of $6.36.

▶ The fourth line shows that $6.36 has been debited to the GST Paid account. GST Paid has increased by $6.36, and at the end of the BAS period this amount will be claimed back from the government (as we will see on day 7).

I know what some of you are thinking: why is a withdrawal from the business cheque account a credit to the business?

One of the first concepts students of bookkeeping need to get their head around is the nature of debit (DR) and credit (CR). Debit and credit are fundamental to the double-entry bookkeeping system. They are used instead of plus (+) and minus (–) symbols to describe increases and decreases in an account, but debit doesn't always mean a decrease and credit doesn't always mean an increase.

The crucial point that you need to understand is that these terms have a specific meaning in relation to particular types of accounts. An entry in the business's accounts that increases an asset or an expense (including cost of sales), or an entry that decreases a liability, equity or income, is a debit. An entry that increases a liability, equity or income, or an entry that decreases an asset or an expense (including cost of sales), is a credit. It's not appropriate to think of a debit or a credit as being good or bad. They are simply accounting concepts. For every transaction, the total of all debits must equal the total of all credits.

Table 2.4 shows how debits and credits apply to different types of accounts.

Table 2.4: nature of debits and credits in relation to different types of accounts

Account	Increase	Decrease
Asset	DR	CR
Liability	CR	DR
Equity	CR	DR
Income	CR	DR
Cost of sales	DR	CR
Expenses	DR	CR
Other Income	CR	DR
Other Expenses	DR	CR

If you look back at the journal entry shown in figure 2.8 (on p. 69), you will see that when office stationery was purchased the cheque account is decreased by $70. The cheque account has been credited by $70. When you look at the cheque statement, the $70 would be in the debit column, because the cheque statement is reflecting the bank's position, not your business's position, in relation to the transaction. Your business's cheque account is a liability to the bank — the bank owes you money. So when the bank's liability is reduced, it is reflected as a debit.

Therefore, a withdrawal from the business cheque account is a credit to the business.

Creating a Spend Money entry

As we noted earlier, the Data Entry Panel of the Bank Register window (see figure 2.6 on p. 68) allows you to quickly record a transaction in MYOB. It's important to note that if a bill has been created through Enter Purchases via the Purchases Command Centre, it cannot be paid for via Spend Money.

We will now work through the steps involved in entering a Spend Money transaction to learn how to enter a simple transaction.

To access the Spend Money window (see figure 2.9), click the Banking Command Centre and then click Spend Money.

Figure 2.9: Banking Command Centre: Spend Money window (example 1)

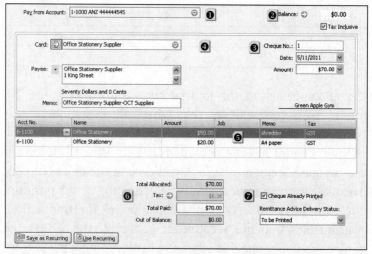

▶ A drop-down list at top left of the Spend Money window allows you select the account from which the money will be paid. Only general ledger accounts that have been linked to the account types Bank or Credit Card will appear on this list. (We touched on this on day 1 when we discussed the chart of accounts.)

▶ Click the drop-down arrow beside the Pay from Account field (see figure 2.10 ❶) and select '1-1000 ANZ 444444545'.

Figure 2.10 ❶: Spend Money window (detail)

On the right-hand side of this field you will see the balance of the selected account and a check box option to indicate whether the transaction is Tax Inclusive or not. For this entry, be sure to tick the Tax Inclusive box (see figure 2.11 ❷).

Figure 2.11 ❷: Spend Money window (detail)

Also on the right you will see the Cheque No., Date and Amount fields (see figure 2.12 ❸).

Figure 2.12 ❸: Spend Money window (detail)

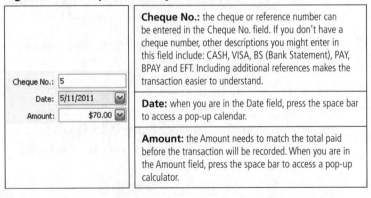

Cheque No.: the cheque or reference number can be entered in the Cheque No. field. If you don't have a cheque number, other descriptions you might enter in this field include: CASH, VISA, BS (Bank Statement), PAY, BPAY and EFT. Including additional references makes the transaction easier to understand.

Date: when you are in the Date field, press the space bar to access a pop-up calendar.

Amount: the Amount needs to match the total paid before the transaction will be recorded. When you are in the Amount field, press the space bar to access a pop-up calculator.

▶ Tab across to the Cheque No. field. The cheque number may already be 1; if not, overtype it and change it to 1.

▶ Tab to the date field and enter 5/11/XX.

▶ Tab to the Amount field and enter $70.

▶ Moving down, you will see the Supplier field details (see figure 2.13 ❹).

Figure 2.13 ❹: Spend Money window (detail)

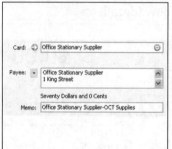

Card: the Card field is where you select the Payee's card. Once a card has been selected, certain information in some fields will fill out automatically. This field can be left blank; you don't need to create a card for every transaction.

Payee: the Payee's address information appears in the Payee field. Up to five different addresses can be selected.

Memo: the memo field can be edited and will appear in various reports.

▶ Click the Card field, select the Office Stationery Supplier card you created on day 1, and tab twice. Data from the card filters through and fills out the Payee field.

▶ Tab through to the Memo field, select the End button, and type '-OCT Supplies'.

▶ Below the first Memo field you can separate out the details of the purchase and allocate them to the appropriate account code (see figure 2.14 ❺). You can also add a job code and a memo. If necessary you can override the default tax code.

Turbo Tip

Assigning job codes to individual transactions enables you to track income and expenses and produce job-specific profit and loss reports.

Figure 2.14 ❺: Spend Money window (detail)

Acct No.	Name	Amount	Job	Memo	Tax
6-1100	Office Stationery	$50.00		shredder	
6-1100	Office Stationery	$20.00		A4 Paper	

▶ Tab to the centre box, and '6-1100' should appear automatically. This is because we defined it as an expense account for Office Stationery Supplies on day 1.

▶ Tab through and enter $50 in the Amount column.

▶ Tab twice to the Memo column and enter 'shredder', then tab across to the Tax column. The tax code for Office Stationery is GST and it should appear automatically. If it doesn't, select it from the drop-down list. We set this up on day 1, when we created the general ledger code 6-1100.

▶ Tab down to the next line, then tab across to the Amount column and enter $20. Tab across to the Memo column and enter 'A4 paper'.

▶ The next section (see figure 2.15 ❻, overleaf) shows the Spend Money totals.

Figure 2.15 ❻: Spend Money window (detail)

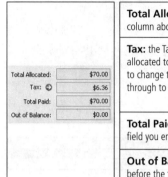

	Total Allocated: the Total Allocated is the sum of the column above.
	Tax: the Tax automatically calculates tax from the tax codes allocated to each individual line. The zoom arrow allows you to change the tax amount, but don't use it, as it won't feed through to your BASlink (see day 7).
	Total Paid: the Total Paid field is the figure from the Amount field you entered in the top right-hand corner.
	Out of Balance: the item Out of Balance needs to be zero before the transaction can be recorded.

The printing options are shown at bottom right (see figure 2.16 ❼).

Figure 2.16 ❼: Spend Money window (detail)

Cheque Already Printed: on day 1 we set the Preferences to default to 'Cheque Already Printed' (see figure 1.30 on p. 27). Otherwise, the cheques would accumulate in your data file waiting to be printed.

Click Record to record the transaction.

Creating a recurring transaction

Let's now work through an example and create a transaction for rent in Spend Money. A timesaving trick for regular transactions is to save the transaction as a recurring template that can be used as needed.

Recurring Transactions can be set up for Sales, Purchases, Spend Money and Receive Money, but they cannot be set up for properly processed payroll payments. Even though you create a transaction template, when you actually use it you can override every aspect of the transaction, from the date to the amount, to where it is allocated. Setting up a recurring transaction in MYOB AccountRight should reduce data processing time and improve productivity.

▶ Enter the following Spend Money transaction for Rent (see figure 2.17).

Figure 2.17: Banking Command Centre: Spend Money window (example 2)

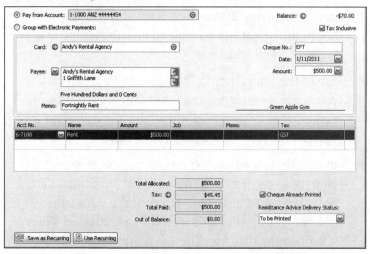

▶ Once all the data has been entered, click the Save as Recurring button at bottom left, and the Recurring Schedule Information window opens (see figure 2.18, overleaf).

Figure 2.18: Recurring Schedule Information window

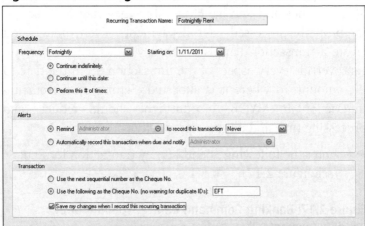

► In the Recurring Transaction Name field, enter Fortnightly Rent. It's sensible to give the template a name you will recall easily.

► Tab to the Frequency field and select Fortnightly. If you select a frequency, the information feeds into the cash flow analysis report. If you don't know when the transaction will occur again, select Never.

► In the Alerts section, you can set up a reminder to yourself to record the transaction on a specified date, or you can set the system to record the transaction automatically. Automatic recording is activated when you open the data file. There is a drawback to using either of these options, however. First, if you set a reminder to yourself and a different user operates the system, that person will not be alerted to the need to process the transaction. Second, if the MYOB data file is set to record automatically and is opened several times on the one day, it will record the transaction each time. So I usually opt for no reminder.

▶ In the Transaction section, I opt for 'Use the following as the Cheque No.' and if appropriate select a reference from the following options: CASH, VISA, BS (Bank Statement), PAY, BPAY.

▶ I usually check the box 'Save my changes when I record this recurring transaction', as this in effect keeps the template up-to-date. If, for example, I enter a different amount the next time I use this recurring transaction, the new amount will be saved and will appear when I open the screen on following occasions.

▶ Once you are satisfied with the template you have created, click OK. You will remember that we explored the Menu Bar on day 1. Menu Bar → Lists → Recurring Transactions is the only place to edit, delete or copy recurring transactions—remember this! (I find that many people are unaware of this option and end up creating masses of unnecessary templates.)

▶ Note that when you save a Recurring Transaction template, it does *not* mean that the original transaction has been recorded. To record the actual transaction, click the Record button.

Exercise 2.2

Go to the Banking Command Centre and click Spend Money, then click Use Recurring at bottom left. The Select a Recurring Transaction window will open up. Double-click Fortnightly Rent. Change the date to 14/11/20XX, and select Record.

Exercise 2.3

Go to the Bank Register and find the fortnightly rental payment to Andy's Rental Agency.

Then go to the Transaction Journal, under the Disbursements tab, and find the fortnightly rental payment to Andy's Rental Agency.

Receiving money

Sales that are not being tracked on a credit basis can be entered through the Receive Money window, which is accessed from the Banking Command Centre. If, however, a sale has been created through the option Enter Sales in the Sales Command Centre, payment cannot be received via Receive Money.

The Receive Money window (see figure 2.19) is very similar to the Spend Money window, although some of the words are slightly different, reflecting the different nature of the transaction.

Figure 2.19: Banking Command Centre: Receive Money window

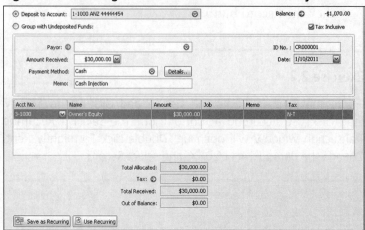

The main difference between the Spend Money and the Receive Money screen is the Payment Method field towards the top of the screen (see figure 2.20).

Figure 2.20: Payment Method field

Payment Method: this field allows you to select the payment method. You can also add details such as the cheque number by clicking on the Details button (see figure 2.11 on p. 78) beside the payment method field. This information feeds into the bank deposit report, which if accepted by your bank will save you time when you are preparing a bank deposit.

If you look back at the Banking Command Centre flowchart (see figure 2.1 on p. 60), after Receive Money you will see the Print Receipts option. Click the Print Receipts button to open the Review Receipts Before Printing window (see figure 2.21, overleaf). This option allows you to print receipts from either Receive Money or Receive Payments. The receipt can be customised and can then be given to the payer.

You can create, edit and delete Payment Methods by accessing the Menu Bar and clicking on Lists → Sales & Purchases Information → Payment Methods. You may find it useful to add payment methods you commonly use such as Direct Deposit.

Figure 2.21: Banking Command Centre: Review Receipts Before Printing window

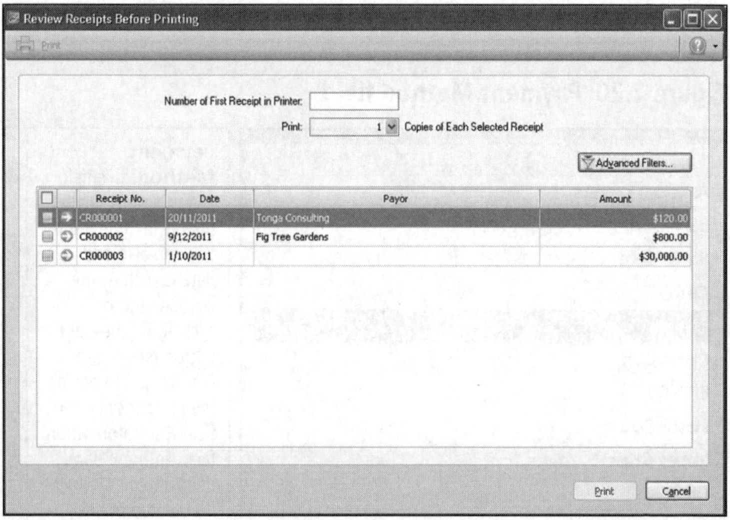

The Advanced Filters button at top right allows you to set criteria for the receipts that need to be printed. Tick the check box on the left beside the individual items you wish to print and then click the Print button at bottom right of the screen.

Exercise 2.4

On 1 October the owner injected $30 000 into the business's ANZ bank account. Use Receive Money and allocate the payment to '3-1000 Owners Equity account'.

Exercise 2.5

Enter the Telstra payment data from figure 2.6 (p. 68), Bank Register Data Entry Panel.

Using the Undeposited Funds account and preparing a bank deposit

If you accept various payments through the day, you may want to select the Undeposited Funds account when receipting payment. The information in this section will give you an overview of how this account is used, but we will not work through a detailed example, as I don't see many businesses using this feature. You can use this account to record the details of daily transactions and then transfer the batch total to the bank account. As you process payments through the day, select the Group with Undeposited Funds account to receipt the payments (see figure 2.22). This option is found at the top of both the Receive Money window (see figure 2.19 on p. 80) and Receive Payment window (see figure 3.14 on p. 112 in day 3).

Figure 2.22: Group with Undeposited Funds option

○	Deposit to Account
◉	Group with Undeposited Funds: 1-2000 Undeposited Funds account

At the end of the day, the bookkeeper counts the cash and cheques to be deposited at the bank and usually places them in a bank satchel. You then need to select the Prepare Bank Deposit button, and the transactions you see on the Prepare Bank Deposit screen should match what is in the bank satchel. Use the Deposit Adjustment button you will see at bottom left to record additional fees or excess funds.

Select all transactions to be deposited and then select the print option at top right. This will result in the transaction being recorded and save you time, as you are printing the bank deposit slip to accompany the bank satchel and don't need to write it out again. When a transaction in MYOB is printed, it is automatically recorded. If bank deposits are received by the business, this process aids in preparing bank reconciliations. The multiple transactions are recorded in the Undeposited Funds account and transferred as a batch entry to the banking account, matching the actual bank deposit.

Preparing electronic payments

In MYOB you can select payments to be processed via electronic banking. You create a file for this purpose and upload it to the business's bank account. To set up your data file for electronic payments, you need to enter the details of both the business's bank account and the supplier's or employee's bank account. Note that BPAY payments cannot be processed in this way; they need to be processed manually.

To set up details of the bank account from which the payments are going to be made, it's necessary to contact your bank and let them know that you want to upload an '.aba' file generated in MYOB. The bank should provide you with a bank code and a direct-entry user ID, and let you know if you need to include a so-called self-balancing transaction. Go to Accounts Command Centre → Accounts List → Bank Account → Banking tab, click 'I Create Bank Files (ABA) for This Account' and fill in the fields.

To set up details of the supplier's or employee's bank account, go to Card File Command Centre → Cards List → Supplier/ Employee → Payment Details. Under Supplier or Employee Payment Details, change the Payment Method to Electronic in order to access the Payment Details fields.

You need to complete all of this information before payment can be made.

When processing a payment, select the Group with Electronic Payments option (see figure 2.23).

Figure 2.23: Group with Electronic Payments option

○	Pay from Account: 1-1000 Cheque Account
◉	Group with Electronic Payments

The next step is to select the Prepare Electronic Payments button, which is found under the Payroll, Purchases or Banking Command Centre. Check the transactions that you want to process electronically. Don't hit record; go to the top of the screen and hit the Bank File button, which will create a bank file (.aba). Save this file to your desktop. This is the bank file that will be uploaded to your bank for processing payments. The bank should provide you with a security code device and instructions on how to upload bank files and process the payments.

Printing cheques

For those businesses that still use cheques, there is an option to print customised cheques via the Print Cheques button (see figure 2.1 on p. 60). You should bear in mind, however, that electronic funds payment is a cheaper and quicker option, as no stamp or envelope is required and many banks charge a fee to process cheques.

Printing or emailing remittance advices

When processing payments, you have the option of printing or emailing remittance advices notifying the recipient that payment has been made. As with any email notification generated by MYOB, the email address needs to be stored in the relevant card file and MYOB needs to communicate with a **MAPI**-compliant email system. As not all suppliers require a remittance advice, suppliers' preferences can be set under the Buying Details tab on their card.

Turbo Tip

Customise the bottom half of remittance advices to promote all the services that your business offers. Turn suppliers into customers!

Bank reconciliation

The purpose of bank reconciliation is to ensure that your MYOB data file matches what is recorded in your bank statement. In a perfect accounting world this would always be the case, but in reality it rarely is. There are many reasons why an actual bank account does not match an MYOB bank account, such as unpresented cheques, bank interest, bank charges, transactions not entered, transactions entered incorrectly, timing differences and fraud. You need to identify these issues, make the necessary adjustments and reconcile the two accounts.

Bank reconciliations are a lot easier to undertake if they are done on a regular basis. How often you do this will depend on the number of transactions you process. As a minimum, bank reconciliations should be undertaken monthly, but high-volume businesses may conduct them daily. Online banking makes this feasible. If your bank statement is issued quarterly, contact the bank and arrange to have it issued monthly, preferably based on the calendar months.

How to do a bank reconciliation

Go to the Banking Command Centre and click Reconcile Accounts, and the Reconcile Accounts window will open (see figure 2.24). (Figure 2.24 is an example only; you will not have this data in your data file yet.)

Figure 2.24: Banking Command Centre: Reconcile Accounts window

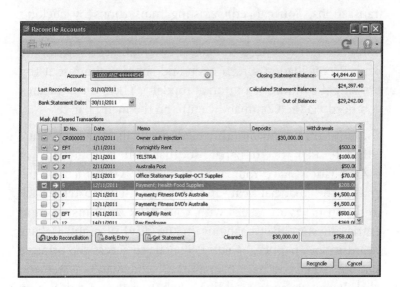

First you need to enter the date in the Bank Statement Date field. Then enter the statement balance from the bank statement in the New Statement Balance. It is important to then tab out of that field so that the action is recognised.

The goal is to reconcile, so the Out of Balance amount should be zero. Sometimes the numbers get 'sticky', so if you think the reconciliation should balance and it doesn't, tab through the two fields again to refresh the calculation.

I suggest that you reconcile transactions in your bank reconciliation methodically, one by one in date order. This allows you to see that the running balance matches the calculated statement balance. If they don't match, an error has occurred somewhere, and you need to revisit the transactions you have just reconciled.

As you work through the bank reconciliation, you may realise that you need to edit some transactions or add new transactions. You can edit existing transactions by clicking on the white zoom arrow and drilling down to the original transaction. If you need to enter a new transaction, leave the Bank Reconciliation screen open and simply minimise it (by pressing the Minimise button at top left). Then select the area you need via the Command Centre on the menu bar.

You must print your monthly bank reconciliation statements, either to PDF or to paper, so that you have a copy at reconciliation date. Your accountant may want them at the end of the financial year, and they are useful to refer back to if you have any issues with your bank accounts, such as entries mysteriously changing in the dead of night. (I have heard it does happen.) Click Reconcile to access the printing options. After you have printed the reconciliation statement, click Reconcile again, and then click it again—yes, it is a bit confusing!

Bank reconciliation: extra options

At bottom left of the Reconcile Accounts window (see figure 2.24 on p. 87) you will see three buttons, Undo Reconciliation, Bank Entry and Get Statement.

The Undo Reconciliation button will undo the reconciliations, starting at the last reconciliation processed and working backwards. You need to take care, as there is not a redo option. Once an account has been undone it needs to be re-reconciled, and the transactions are not even ticked to indicate that they were reconciled, as you may assume they would be.

The Bank Entry button at bottom left of the screen allows you to enter bank charges or interest. These will automatically be ticked as reconciled.

The Get Statement button allows you to import bank or credit card statements, thereby speeding up the reconciliation process.

Resolving bank reconciliation issues

If you have issues resolving your bank reconciliation, *Learn Bookkeeping in 7 Days* by Rod Caldwell (see resources on p. 288) covers the process of manual bank reconciliation in detail.

There are various areas you need to check to resolve any issues.

▶   Check that all transactions have been entered.

▶   Check that the opening balance is correct. If it isn't, you will need to go back to prior periods to establish when it was correct and in this way identify the month in which the error was introduced.

▶   Check that the new statement balance you entered is correct.

▶   Think back to see if you can remember making any changes to historical data after you reconciled, and investigate further.

▶   Identify the Out of Balance amount. Does it ring any bells? Can you think of anything it might relate to? Search for the Out of Balance amount in the Find Transactions area of the Command Panel.

We will work through a bank reconciliation exercise on day 7.

What is an audit trail, and why is it important?

An audit trail is a chronological step-by-step path of evidence of a financial transaction and who was responsible for dealing with the transaction. It can help to reveal whether misappropriation has occurred.

For the Audit Trail in MYOB AccountRight to work effectively, all users should access the software using their own user names and passwords. There are two audit trail reports: Under Reports → Accounts → Security and Audit, you will find the Journal Security Audit and Session Security Audit Report. These reports track changes made to transactions, accounts and some system settings, plus the ID of the user who made the changes. Another useful audit trail report is the General Journal report, which can be customised to show all transactions, session dates and user IDs.

Use the owner's loan account to monitor the owner's spending

On day 1 we set up the account '2-9000 Loan—Owner's Name' to process business items the business owner paid for personally (see figure 1.40 on p. 45). I recommend that you set up the Owner's Loan Account in the Liabilities area as a Credit Card type account. If the account has a positive balance, the business owes the owner money, and if the balance is negative, the owner owes the business money.

The following is a common scenario: the owner is at the post office and uses $50 cash to buy stamps. You can enter this transaction through Spend Money, as shown in figure 2.25. Note that '2-9000 Loan — Owner's Name' is selected in the Pay from Account field and that the rest of the transaction looks like a straightforward Spend Money transaction — a purchase of stamps at Australia Post. If the scenario were different and the owner was receiving money from the business for personal use, you would process this transaction through Receive Money and use the account '2-9000 Loan — Owner's Name' to receipt it.

Figure 2.25: Spend Money window: Australia Post payment

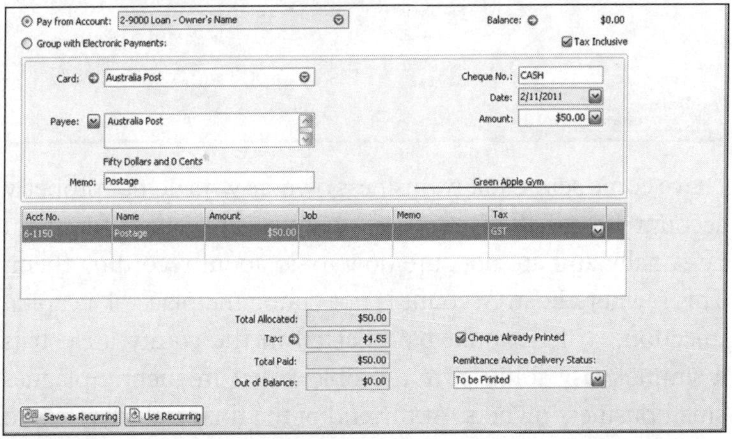

Another benefit of setting up an Owner's Loan Account is that if the payment made by the business is partially personal, the loan account can be used to apportion the personal component. This is shown in figure 2.26 (overleaf): a payment is made to Telstra for a telephone account expense, but 20 per cent of the telephone usage is deemed personal and allocated to the Owner's Loan Account. Note that the payment is made from the business bank account.

Figure 2.26: Spend Money window: Telstra payment (80 per cent business/20 per cent personal)

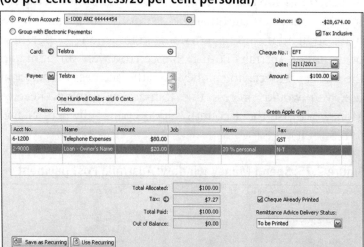

I have come across many business owners who do not properly account for all their expenses, because they paid for them personally and are not sure how to go about recording them. This Owner's Loan Account is not taking the place of a capital injection, which would be reflected in the equity area. It is a simple, easy solution to a problem that frequently plagues small business owners. At the end of the financial year, aim to run the Owner's Loan Account to zero so as not to complicate any equity or ownership matters.

Exercise 2.6

Enter the data from figure 2.25 (on p. 91), Spend Money window: Australia Post payment, and figure 2.26, Spend Money window: Telstra payment. Note that no GST is accrued on the personal component of the expenditure.

Summary of day 2

On day 2 we explored the Banking Command Centre, building on what we learned on day 1. We discussed the fundamental accounting concepts of cash accounting and accrual-based accounting. It is important that the business selects and applies these accounting methods consistently across their books to ensure reporting accuracy. Also included in this day was a useful table defining the nature of debits and credits for different types of accounts. You may refer back to this table as you progress through the week. We were introduced to the purpose of linked accounts within MYOB. You have learned how to enter cash transactions in Spend Money and Receive Money and where to find transactions in the Bank Register and the Transaction Journal. We covered several time-saving techniques including setting up recurring transactions, using the undeposited funds account for multiple receipts, and setting up the electronic payment feature for multiple payments. You have also been introduced to the concept of bank reconciliations, and you should now recognise the importance of undertaking reconciliations regularly to ensure the accuracy of your data. On day 3 we will explore the Sales Command Centre and learn how to raise invoices, receipt payments and analyse sales.

Day 3

Sales Command Centre

Key terms and concepts

▶ *Trade debtors:* the amount of money due from customers.

▶ *Sales register:* a record of all sales activities, including open and closed invoices, quotes, orders, and returns and credits.

▶ *Transaction journal:* a list of all journal entries—General, Disbursements, Receipts, Sales, Purchases and Inventory journals.

Introduction and overview

Day 3 introduces you to the Sales Command Centre (see figure 3.1, overleaf). This area of MYOB is a favourite among small business owners, for obvious reasons. This is where you raise invoices for goods or services, receipt payments against **trade debtors**, and monitor accounts receivable. Today we will discuss the Sales Linked Accounts window and look at the different stages of a sale and different sales layouts; visit the Sales Register and the Transaction Journal; and enter and receive payments against different sales.

Figure 3.1: Sales Command Centre flowchart

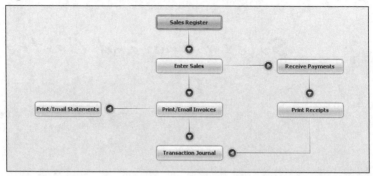

I have come across numerous businesses that use MYOB just for creating sales invoices to issue to customers. If this applies to you, you now have the opportunity to learn how to receipt payments and track outstanding invoices as well. Receiving payment for just one invoice that may in the past have gone unnoticed may well pay for the time and effort you have spent learning MYOB this week. Also, don't be the person who celebrates a sale three times: when the job is completed, when the invoice is raised, and when the payment is received. You are in business to make money and you can celebrate when payment is in the bank account. The primary goal of the Sales Command Centre is to ensure that this happens.

Linked accounts

The Sales Command Centre has its own linked accounts similar to the linked accounts we discussed on day 2. To view these accounts, go to Setup → Linked Accounts, and the Sales Linked Accounts window will open (see figure 3.2).

Figure 3.2: Sales Linked Accounts window

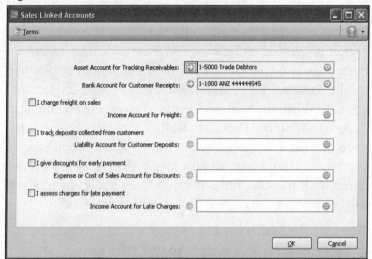

The first two links relate to how accrual sales are processed in MYOB. Don't be freaked out by the word 'accrual'. As we discussed on day 2, it simply means we are tracking receipts that are due, not recording them on the day they are received. When a sale is recorded through the Sales Command Centre, the asset account Trade Debtors is used to record the amount receivable. When a payment is receipted against the sale, the amount is transferred from the Trade Debtors account to the Bank account. The sequence is as follows:

Sale raised → Trade Debtors account → Bank account.

There are four other lines in the Sales Linked Accounts window, and it is really up to you whether your business utilises these options. The terminology is self-explanatory. If you are creating a file from scratch, you may need to set up the underlying accounts.

Your existing data file will not have the last four boxes linked. The only tricky linked account here that is worth a mention is the option 'I track deposits collected from customers'. If this option is selected and a customer pays a deposit against an open sales quote or sales order, then the deposit is allocated to the clearing account known as the Deposits Liability account. When the final payment is received, the accumulated deposits within the Deposits Liability account are transferred to reduce the Trade Debtors account. That may sound a little complicated, but essentially, if a sales order is raised, a deposit is received, the sales order is turned into a sales invoice and the full amount is received, then it will work smoothly.

However, if you don't or can't adhere to that process because, as happens, deposits are received and sales invoices are then cancelled, the mechanisms for dealing with this get a little complicated. The sales invoice and the deposit received cannot be deleted and need to be reversed. For this reason I usually advise my clients to keep it simple and not to select the option 'I track deposits collected from customers'. If you do select this option and run into difficulties, you will need to carefully identify the flow of transactions and go backwards through them and reverse them, until you are able to correctly represent what actually happened.

Types of sales

The three stages of sales records that can be created in MYOB—quote, order and invoice—are referred to as types of sales. Each type (or stage) is distinguished by a colour: salmon pink for sales quotes, yellow for sales orders and pale powdery blue for sales invoices. (The colours are quite faint and can be hard to see.) A *sales quote* does not create a transaction and leads to no further action within the system. A *sales order* does not create a transaction but will place a hold on inventory ordered. The sales quote and sales order will remain in MYOB until they are converted to an *invoice* or deleted. When a sale is created against the relevant customer, a reminder window will pop up and existing sales quotes or sales orders can be selected.

To select different types of sales, go to the Sales Command Centre and click the Enter Sales button. Then click the drop-down arrow in the Sales Type field at top left to select from the three options: Quote, Order and Invoice.

Sales layouts

MYOB gives you a choice of five sales layouts to suit different purposes: Service, Item, Professional, Time Billing and Miscellaneous. Most businesses would need only one layout for the bulk of their transactions and use the others occasionally.

▶ The Service layout is a standard style of invoice used to detail services and non-inventoried **stock**. It can also be used as a default invoice when none of the other styles is appropriate.

▶ The Item layout is used for sales of inventoried stock. This layout is suitable for businesses that sell stock of any type.

▶ The Professional layout is similar to the Service layout except that there is no 'Ship to' field and there is a column for listing the date on which the service was provided. This layout is appropriate for contractors who wish to provide details of the services they provided against the date they worked.

▶ If you are using Activity Slips or Timesheets in MYOB, the details can feed into the Time Billing invoice layout, or you can create this type as a stand-alone invoice that links to chargeable Activities. This layout is appropriate for consultants who charge out their time. Activity Slips and Timesheets will not be covered in this book.

▶ The Miscellaneous layout is used for **bad debts** and miscellaneous administrative purposes. This layout cannot be printed.

The Sales layout can be pre-selected in the Customer Card under the Selling Details tab, and when the customer is selected in the Sales window the layout will also appear. To access the different layouts, go to the Sales Command Centre and click the Enter Sales button, then click the Layout button and choose from the five options.

Exercise 3.1

Go to the Sales Command Centre and click the Enter Sales button. Spend some time familiarising yourself with the different types of sales (quote, order and invoice) and the five different sales layouts (Service, Item, Professional, Time Billing and Miscellaneous).

Sales Register and Transaction Journal

The Sales Register can be used to create sales quotes and sales invoices, to convert sales quotes and sales orders to sales invoices, and to receipt payments. The Sales Register Information window (see figure 3.3) has six tabs: All Sales, Quotes, Orders, Open Invoices, Returns and Credits, and Closed Invoices. (Figures 3.3 and 3.4 on p. 102 are examples only; there will be no transactions in your data file.) Under the Returns and Credits tab, if a Sale is reversed, an adjustment note is issued, or an overpayment is made, a refund can be paid to the client or applied against existing sales. If you are using an historical MYOB data file, check under the Returns and Credits tab to see if there are any historical transactions you need to deal with.

Figure 3.3: Sales Register Information window

When you are looking for transactions, first make sure you have selected the relevant date range. To see all of the information on an invoice, hover over Invoice No. 3, Cash Sale, for example, and double-click it, or click the zoom arrow to drill down to see the information on the invoice. Hover near the top of the invoice and right-click your mouse to bring up a context-sensitive menu. While you are here, select Delete Sale. The invoice is deleted and you return to the Sales Register Information window (see figure 3.3).

The Sales tab under the Transaction Journal window (see figure 3.4, overleaf) details Sales in journal format. If you are familiar with journal entries and find it easier to understand the transaction by looking at the debit and credit movements, or you are querying an entry, it's useful to look here to see the different accounts that the transaction has been posted to.

Figure 3.4: Transaction Journal window

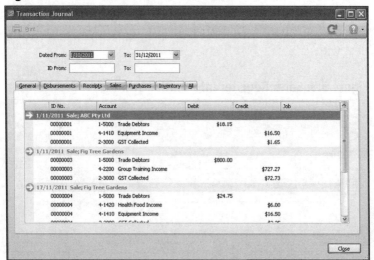

Notice that each transaction results in the Trade Debtors account being debited for the total value of the sale. Any payment received for a sale can be viewed under the Receipts tab, and typically the amount will be transferred from Trade Debtors to the Bank account, as defined in the Sales Linked Accounts.

Entering sales

I cannot emphasise enough that sales need to be entered in a timely fashion. I also encourage you to include as much information as possible on the sales invoice. This information is not only an aid to decision making but will also be useful as supporting evidence when debts are being collected.

Include details such as authorised purchase orders and activity slips, dates, the people involved, the goods provided and the expenses incurred.

Creating a Service Type sale

▶ To create a new sale, click the Sales Command Centre and then Enter Sales, and the Sales window will open.

▶ Start to type in the customer name, ABC Pty Ltd, in the Customer field at top left, and a drop-down list will appear. When you select the relevant customer name, the layout will change to Service (assuming that the Service window is not already open), as shown in figure 3.5, Sales: Edit Service window. Various fields, including 'Ship to', Terms, Salesperson, Shipping Via and Invoice Delivery Status will fill out from the Customer Card if they have been set up as default options. (You learned how to set up Customer Card information on day 1.) This saves you a considerable amount of processing time when dealing with regular clients.

Figure 3.5: Sales: Edit Service window

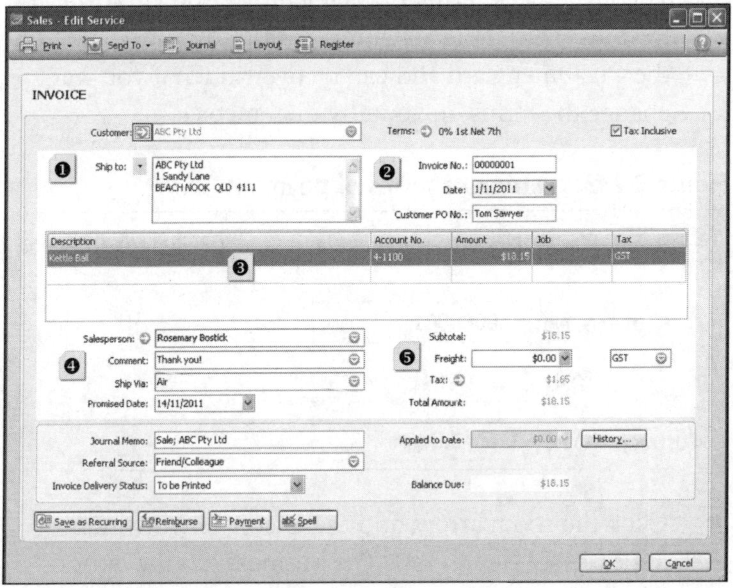

You can change the 'Ship to' address (see figure 3.6 ❶) by clicking the drop-down arrow and selecting the required address from the Customer Card's five address fields. Alternatively, you can select an address from a different Customer Card. This is useful when the products are delivered to different stores but the invoice goes to head office.

Figure 3.6 ❶: 'Ship to' address field

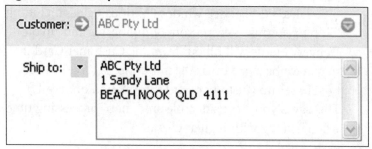

The customer's terms of payment are shown at the top towards the right (see figure 3.7 ❷). They originate from the Customer Card and can be overridden if you want to change the terms on an individual invoice.

Figure 3.7 ❷: customer's terms of payment

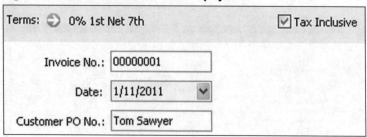

▶ Click the zoom arrow, and the Credit Terms window appears (see figure 3.8). The business has the option of offering a discount for early payment and applying

finance charges for late payment. Click the field
Payment is Due and select On a Given No. of Days, and
then enter the number 7 in the Balance Due Date field.
The invoice will now include a request to the customer
to pay in seven days. Click OK and note that the terms
have changed to Net 7.

Figure 3.8: Credit Terms window

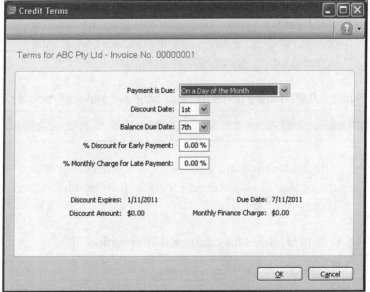

▶ If you look again at figure 3.7 ❷, the customer's terms
of payment, below the terms you will see the Invoice
No. field. This fills out automatically, following on
from the previous invoice number created. The invoice
number field can be overridden—so if, for example,
you entered the invoice number 400, when the next sale
was created it would be numbered 401.

▶ The next field is a standard Date field, and below that
is a field for the customer purchase order (PO) number.

If you don't have a PO number, enter the name of the client who is authorising the purchase.

In our scenario, the business is selling ABC Pty Ltd one kettlebell.

▶ Tab across to the Description column (figure 3.9 ❸) and enter 'Kettlebell'. Tab across to the Account No. column, and the account number 4-1100 (which is linked to Fitness Equipment Sales) should automatically appear (see figure 3.5 on p. 103). Tab across to the Amount column and enter $18.15. The tax code GST should automatically appear.

Figure 3.9 ❸: middle panel of Sales window: Service Type sale

Description	Account No.	Amount	Job	Tax	
Kettlebell	4-1100	$18.15		GST	

▶ The fields at bottom right of the sales invoice give you the option of collecting a variety of further information (figure 3.10 ❹).

Figure 3.10 ❹: fields for additional information

Salesperson:	Rosemary Bostick
Comment:	Thank you!
Ship Via:	Air
Promised Date:	14/11/2011
Journal Memo:	Sale; ABC Pty Ltd
Referral Source:	Friend/Colleague
Invoice Delivery Status:	To be Printed

You can enter the salesperson's name, but only if you have previously set up an Employee Card for that person. If you have salespeople working as contractors, you may need to set them up as dummy employees. These links to employees generate a collection of sales reports, located under Reports → Sales → Salesperson, which can be used to motivate and reward individual salespeople.

- The Comment field allows you to add a note to the sales invoice.
- The Ship Via field is self-explanatory.
- The Promised Date is the date scheduled for delivery of the goods or service to the customer.
- The Journal Memo field automatically generates the word Sale followed by a semi-colon and the customer name. This information can be overridden if you wish.
- If you enter the Referral Source, reports can be generated to indicate sales related to a particular referral source.
- The Invoice Delivery Status field allows you to select how the form is to be delivered to the customer—via a printed copy or email. If a printed copy is not required, select 'Already Printed or Sent'.

▶ Enter the data as shown in figure 3.5 (on p. 103). At bottom right the sales invoice has a field for the Subtotal, which is automatically calculated (see figure 3.11 ❺, overleaf).

▶ Click Record to record the sales transaction.

Figure 3.11 ❺: Sales: Edit Service window (detail)

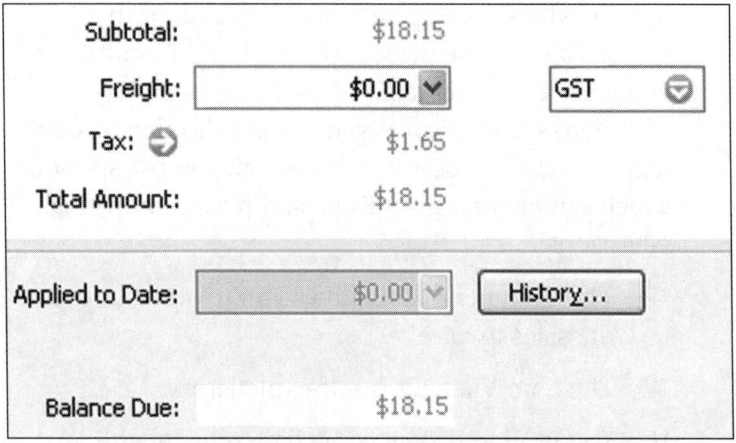

Subtotal:	$18.15	
Freight:	$0.00 ⌄	GST ⌄
Tax: ⊙	$1.65	
Total Amount:	$18.15	
Applied to Date:	$0.00 ⌄	History...
Balance Due:	$18.15	

⌷ The Tax field automatically calculates the tax from the tax codes linked to individual transaction lines.

⌷ There is an option to record any amount Paid Today, but the payment will only be deposited in the bank account linked to the Bank Account for Customer Receipts, as shown in the Sales Linked Accounts window (see figure 3.2 on p. 97).

⌷ There is a field to enter the Payment Method, and you can add further information by clicking on the Details tab.

Pre-defined options are available for the Comment, Ship Via, Referral Source and Payment Method fields (see figure 3.5 on p. 103). Alternative options can be added directly to the Sales invoice and will be added to the option list. All available options in the Comment, Ship Via, Referral Source and Payment Method fields can only be edited via Menu Bar → Lists → Sales and Purchases Information.

Creating a Professional Type sale

As noted previously, the layout of Professional sales is similar
to that of Service sales. The main difference is in the centre bar
of the Professional sales layout, which includes a date column.

▶   To start, we need to mark Tonga Consulting as active.
    Go to the Card File Command Centre and click Card
    List. Double click Tonga Consulting and untick the
    Inactive Card field at the top right-hand corner. Click
    OK.

▶   To create a new sale, click the Sales Command Centre and
    then Enter Sales, and the Sales window will open. The
    sale layout that appears will be the type last used. Type
    Tonga Consulting in the Customer field and tab through.
    A Professional-style sales layout will appear, as this is the
    default sales layout for this customer (see figure 3.12).

Figure 3.12: Sales: Edit Professional window

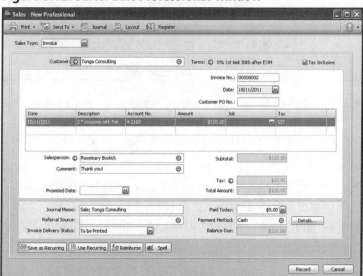

To verify this, click the white zoom arrow on the left-hand side of the Customer field to drill down to the Customer Card. Click the third tab at the top, Selling Details, and the first field that appears is Sale Layout, as shown in figure 3.13. If a default option has not previously been selected, the Customer Card will be created with a 'No Default' option. If a default format was selected during set-up or when the Customer Card was created, then that format will appear when the customer is selected, but it can be overridden.

Figure 3.13: Customer Card: Selling Details tab

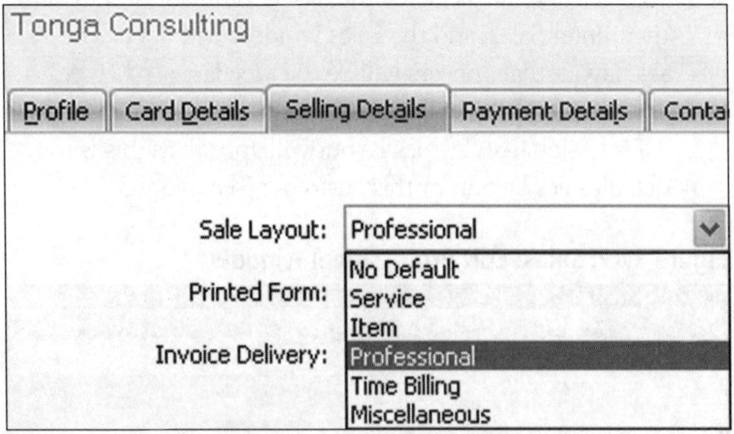

Tonga Consulting

| Profile | Card Details | Selling Details | Payment Details | Conta |

Sale Layout: Professional

No Default
Service
Item
Professional
Time Billing
Miscellaneous

Printed Form:

Invoice Delivery:

▶   Click the OK button at bottom right of the Customer Card to return to the Sales window (see figure 3.12 on p. 109). Tab through and change the date to 18/11/20XX.

▶   In the same window, type the date 10/11/20XX in the centre panel. This is the date on which the service was provided. Tab through to the Description column and type in '2 * sessions with Pat'. Then tab through to the Account No. field and click the small drop-down arrow to the right of the column, and the Account Number and Name will appear. Select '4-2100 Income–1on1 Fitness Class Income'. GST should automatically appear in the Tax column, as it is the default tax code for this account. Tab through and enter $120 in the Amount column.

▶ On day 1 we covered how to use Preferences on the Menu Bar under Setup. If you find the account number on the sales form confusing, you can opt to have the account name appear instead. Go to Menu Bar → Setup → Preferences → Windows tab and tick the check box beside Select and Display Account Name, Not Number.

▶ Fill out the remaining invoice fields from the information shown in figure 3.12 (on p. 109), and click the Record button.

Receiving payments

By using the Receive Payments button, you can apply payments received from customers against open invoices.

As we discussed on day 2, if the sale is created through the Sales Command Centre, the money must be receipted through Receive Payments.

▶ To enter a receipt, go to the Sales Command Centre and click Receive Payments, and the Receive Payments window will open (see figure 3.14, overleaf).

Figure 3.14: Receive Payments window

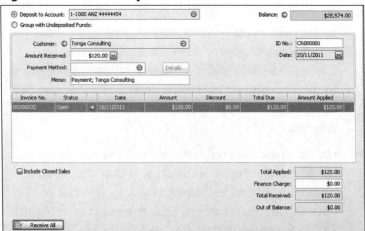

▶ Tab to the first field beside Deposit to Account and select '1-1000 ANZ 44444454' from the drop-down menu. This is the account in which the money was deposited. Start typing the customer's name, Tonga Consulting, in the Customer field. A drop-down menu will appear with details of outstanding balances, and the required customer can be selected from the list. Outstanding invoices will appear in the centre box.

▶ In the Amount Received field, enter $120.

▶ Select Cheque as the Payment Method. You are able to add additional information here, which (as we noted on day 2) is useful for preparing the bank deposit slip. Click the Details button to the left of the Payment Method field, and the Applied Payment Details window will open (see figure 3.10 on p. 106). In the BSB field, enter '444444'; this will automatically be separated by a hyphen. In the Account Name field, enter 'J K Potter'; in the Account No. field, enter '5555555'; and in the Cheque No. field, enter '546'.

Then click the OK button at bottom right of the
Applied Payment Details window (see figure 3.15).

Figure 3.15: Applied Payment Details window

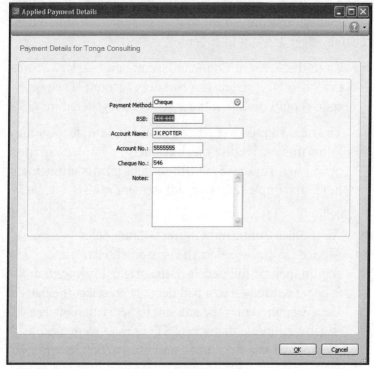

▶ Click Close, and you will return to the Receive
Payments window (see figure 3.14). Tab across to the
Date field and enter 20/11/20XX.

▶ Tab to the first row of the centre box and type
$120 in the Amount Applied column, then tab
through so that the $120 appears in the Total
Applied field below.

▶ Click Record.

Processing a bad debt

Unfortunately, sometimes payment for a sale is not received. Once the business's debt collection procedures have been exhausted, it's necessary to write the bad debt off. A bad debt is a business expense, so the first step is to create a bad debt general ledger account in expenses.

▶ Go to the Account Command Centre and click Accounts List, then New, to create a bad debt account. The tax code should be GST if the business is registered for GST.

The next step is to create an adjustment note. You may know this as a credit note, but since the implementation of GST in Australia in 2000 the official term is 'adjustment note'. In simple terms, an adjustment note is a negative sale.

▶ Go to Sales Command Centre → Enter Sales → Choose Service Layout → Select the Customer. Here you should include full details of the original invoice that is being written off as a bad debt. Then select the Bad Debt account; enter the amount to be written off as a negative; allocate the same GST codes as were used in the original sale document; and finally click Record.

Once you have created the adjustment note, you need to apply it to the original sale. This is processed through the Returns and Credits tab on the Sales Register Information window (see figure 3.3 on p. 101).

▶ Go to Sales Command Centre → Sales Register → Returns and Credits tab. Select Adjustment Note and click the Apply to Sale button. The Settle Returns and Credits window opens. Enter the write-off amount against the original invoice, and then click Record.

Exercise 3.2

1   Fig Tree Gardens has approached Green Apple Gym about providing a fitness instructor for group training sessions at the garden. Create and print a Service Type quote for Fig Tree Gardens using the following details:

- Invoice No: 3

- Date: 1 November 20XX

- Description: Gardens for group training sessions, Mon–Fri, Month of December

- Cost: $800 inclusive of GST

- Salesperson: Rosemary Bostick

- Promised Date: 1 December 20XX

Remember that you will need to create a Customer Card for Fig Tree Gardens and to select a Quote Type sale (the background will be pink).

2   Fig Tree Gardens has received the quote, authorised the purchase and issued a purchase order number: FTOCT369. Change the quote to an invoice and issue it to Fig Tree Gardens.

Go to the Sales Command Centre, click the Sales Register and then click the Quotes tab. Ensure that the date range starts at 1 November 20XX. Click the Fig Tree Gardens quote to highlight it. Go to the bottom, select the Change to Invoice button, and alter the invoice date to 1 December 20XX. Enter the PO number and click Record, then click OK to return to the Sales Command Centre.

3   Fig Tree Gardens paid the full amount of the invoice on 9 December 20XX by bank transfer. Record the payment.

Go to the Sales Command Centre and click Receive Payments. In the Customer field, type in Fig Tree Gardens and tab through. Process the payment against the invoice, make sure Out of Balance is zero, and then click Record.

Reconciling sales

It's a requirement of the bookkeeping process to reconcile sales on a regular basis. The reconciliation involves comparing the outstanding accounts in the Sales Ledger with the Trade Debtors balance. This is an easy operation within MYOB, as you can access a report that compares these two amounts. This is called the Receivables Reconciliation Exceptions report (see figure 3.16) and is found within the Company Data Auditor in the Accounts Command Centre. (We will cover the Company Data Auditor on day 7.) Another way to find this report is to click on Reports, at either the top or bottom of the screen, select Sales → Receivables Reconciliation (Summary) and run the report as at 1/11/XX.

Figure 3.16: Company Data Auditor: Receivables Reconciliation Exceptions report

Name	Total Due	0 - 30	31 - 60	61 - 90	90+
ABC Pty Ltd	$18.15	$18.15	$0.00	$0.00	$0.00
Total:	$18.15	$18.15	$0.00	$0.00	$0.00
Ageing Percent:		100.0%	0.0%	0.0%	0.0%
Receivables Account:	$18.15				
Out of Balance Amount	$0.00				

Green Apple Gym
1 Penny Lane, Orchard Way

Receivables Reconciliation [Summary]
As of 1/11/2011
ABN: 44 554 455 445
Email: green@applegym.com

The Total Amount Outstanding represents the total of open invoices as found in the Sales Ledger, and the Linked Receivables Account Balance reflects the balance of 1-1500, the Trade Debtors account. Ideally they should always be the same, but if a transaction has been posted directly to the Trade Debtors account, or payment for a sale has been receipted through Receive Payments in the Banking Command Centre, they will not reconcile and the transaction needs to be corrected.

Invoice Statements and Activity Statements

A statement is a document summarising outstanding invoices that the business issues to its customers. Some businesses that issue a high volume of invoices per customer—for example, for a daily bread delivery—issue a separate invoice per delivery but may only require payment on receipt of statement. Similarly, some clients may expect to pay only on receipt of statement. You need to make sure that your customers clearly understand when you require payment. Within MYOB there are two types of statements, Activity Statements and Invoice Statements.

The Activity Statement details invoices, orders and receipts that have occurred over a period of time.

The Invoice Statement details open invoices and their balances as at a certain date.

To access the statements, go to the Sales Command Centre and click the Print/Email Statements button. You can then click the Advanced Filters button to generate statements based on your desired criteria. The ageing criterion at the base of the statement is generated from the original invoice.

Analysing receivables

If you are using AccountRight version 19 or above, go to the bottom right-hand corner of the home screen and click the Business Insights button. At bottom left of the Business Insights window you will see a range of Customer Analysis statistics, including the number of customers who owe you money. If you have an earlier version of MYOB, go to the Sales Command Centre and click the Analysis button at bottom right, and the Analyse Receivables window will open. Figure 3.17 shows an extract from the Aged Receivables Summary that can be accessed by clicking on Reports. Select Sales → Aged Receivables (Summary) and run the report as at 1/11/XX.

Figure 3.17: Aged Receivables Summary (extract)

				Green Apple Gym	
Aged Receivables [Summary]				1 Penny Lane, Orchard Way	
As of 1/11/2011				ABN: 44 554 455 445	
				Email: green@applegym.com	
Name	Total Due	0 - 30	31 - 60	61 - 90	90+
ABC Pty Ltd	$18.15	$18.15	$0.00	$0.00	$0.00
Total:	$18.15	$18.15	$0.00	$0.00	$0.00
Ageing Percent:		100.0%	0.0%	0.0%	0.0%

You will quickly see who owes the business, how much they owe and how late the payment is, and so you can use this window to chase outstanding debts. The total amount listed as owed in this window should equal the Trade Debtors account balance.

The ageing criteria can be changed under Setup → Preferences, as we covered on day 1. Different businesses will require different ageing criteria, but I recommend that you set the criteria in such a way that any issues will be highlighted immediately.

As with all reports, it's important when using this window to make sure that the financial information is up-to-date and that all receipts have been applied to the invoices.

Managing debtors in MYOB

It is probably true to say that most small business owners look upon debt collection as a necessary evil. It's something many of us would really rather not do, but we must do it if we want our business to survive.

If debt collection is an issue that concerns you, rest assured that you are not alone. In Flying Solo's 'Understanding Micro Business 2010–2011' survey, 30 per cent of soloists said getting paid is one of the key challenges facing their business. (Flying Solo is a business website for 'solopreneurs'.)

Getting paid for your work upfront is the ideal solution to this age-old problem, but it is not always feasible. Fortunately, however, your MYOB software can assist you in many aspects of the debt collection process.

Credit applications and terms of engagement

MYOB software comes with a Credit Application template letter that you can issue to potential customers who want credit terms with your business. This can be edited to suit the business's requirements. Some fields in the template are automatically filled out from the information on the Customer Card. To create a customised credit application, go to the Card File Command Centre, click Create Personalised Letters, tick the check box beside the relevant Customer, and click the Mail Merge button. A list of templates will appear. Select Credit Application → click Use Template → answer the pop-up questions and, voilà, you have a Credit Application with the customer details pre-filled.

The original templates are located in the Letters folder under the MYOB software directory. After editing them, save them as Word templates into the Letters folder. In my own business I use a terms of engagement or service agreement contract, which outlines the services I provide and the associated costs. I can then auto-fill the contract with customer information from the MYOB AccountRight card file data.

Pricing

It's important to ensure that every customer or client understands the price of your product or service and what is and is not included in your quote. Don't assume that customers have read your promotional material and know how you operate. After you click the Enter Sale button (as a sale starts life as a quote), select Quote from the Sales Type drop-down menu (see figure 3.18). The quote template includes pricing and can include terms and conditions.

Figure 3.18: Sales Type drop-down menu

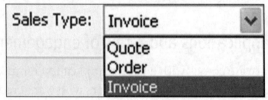

Authorisation

It is good practice always to request a PO number, or the name of the person authorised to approve payment, and to enter this information on the Sales Invoice in the Purchase Order No. field.

Customising invoices

Invoices contain important information, which should be presented in a clear and legible manner. Ensure that your invoices do what they are intended to do — that is, make it clear to your customers how much they owe you, and how and when they need to pay. Invoice templates in MYOB AccountRight can be customised.

Go to Setup and select Customise Forms → Invoices → Service → INCSIPLN-XXXX, click Customise and the Customise Forms window will open (see figure 3.19). Once you have had a look at the options available, exit this window and then click Close to exit the Customise selection area.

Figure 3.19: Customise Forms window

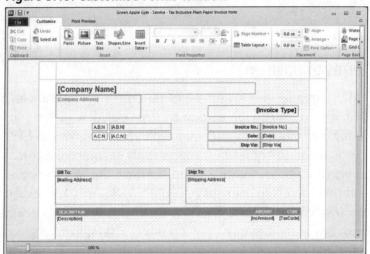

Timely invoices

Send your invoices out as quickly as possible. The sooner your customer receives the invoice, the sooner it will fall due for payment and the healthier your cash flow will be. Invoices can be emailed directly from MYOB software if you are using MAPI-compliant email software. If you are using a cloud email account like gmail or hotmail, the invoice can be converted to PDF and emailed.

Turbo Tip

Two useful freeware (free software) downloads you can access from the internet are CutePDF Writer and ClickYes. CutePDF Writer allows you to print professional-quality PDF files. ClickYes allows MYOB to send email directly to Microsoft Outlook without requesting permission for each individual emailed invoice. This saves time if you are emailing a large batch of invoices or statements from MYOB.

Terms of payment

Think carefully about your payment terms and don't assume that you are stuck with a situation that doesn't work for you. In my own business I initially offered terms of 30 days, as I felt it was the industry norm. Unfortunately, it meant that I had to wait for 30 days until I could start chasing up payments, and that I received many payments 45 days after I had issued the invoice, which was far from ideal for my business cash flow. Over time I reduced my terms to 14 days, then to seven days, and now I ask for payment on the day of service. Today, most of my clients automatically pay me on the day I work for them. My business cash flow is happy, and I have gained back the time I used to spend chasing payments.

The default credit terms are found under Setup → Preferences → Sales. Click the Credit Terms button at top left to set up your business's default credit terms (see figure 3.20).

Figure 3.20: Credit Terms button

All new Customer Cards will now have these credit terms as a default under the Selling Details tab. The credit terms on individual Customer Cards can be edited, so some cards will have customised default credit terms. When you create an invoice for one of these customers, it will automatically reflect the customised default credit terms—and they, too, can be edited.

Following up on unpaid accounts

When you issue an invoice, contact the customer's accounts payable department to confirm that it has been received. You can do this by email, phone or SMS, and it's a friendly and professional touch to make sure that the invoice has been received and has not been lost.

Use the Contact Log found on your Customer Card profile to record this interaction. Click the Customer Card, click the Contact Log tab, and then click the New Log Entry button at the bottom of the screen. Enter the name of the contact you spoke with and brief details of the interaction, and set a re-contact date.

At the appropriate time, contact the customer again to check whether the invoice has been approved for payment, and enter the details in the Contact Log. Keep these conversations friendly and professional; get to know the names of the accounts payable staff and establish a connection with them by chatting about the weather or whatever, as appropriate.

These communications can take place before the invoice is due and will highlight any discrepancies that need to be dealt with. If the staff concerned feel friendly towards you, it is more likely that the accounts payable department will actively process your invoice or at least advise you when you can expect payment.

Once payment is overdue, you can issue an Invoice Statement or Activity Statement to the customer.

Avoid giving clients a reason to delay paying your invoices. If you have adopted these business-savvy guidelines for collecting debt, in most instances you will be paid in a timely fashion. Some invoices may still slip through the cracks, of course, in which case you will need to explore further options.

Summary of day 3

Day 3 has introduced you to the Sales Command Centre: how it is set up, how sales are processed, how money is receipted and how MYOB software can be used to chase outstanding debts. Effective use of this area is essential for a healthy cash flow. On day 4 we will explore the Purchase Command Centre, which is a mirror image of the Sales Command Centre. You will learn how to raise purchases, pay bills and analyse creditors.

Day 4

Purchase Command Centre

Key terms and concepts

▶ *Credit purchase:* a purchase made on credit terms; that is, where the buyer receives goods or services and agrees to pay for them at a later date on the supplier's terms.

▶ *Trade creditor:* a person or business to which the business owes money for purchases made on credit. Also, the name of the account used to record the amount payable.

Introduction and overview

Day 4 introduces you to the Purchase Command Centre (see figure 4.1, overleaf). In this area, purchases are processed on an accruals basis against **trade creditors**; accounts payable are monitored and paid for; and remittance advices are issued. Today we will look at the Purchases Linked Accounts and the various invoice types and layouts. We will then visit the Purchases Register and Transaction Journal and enter and pay for various purchases.

Figure 4.1: Purchase Command Centre flowchart

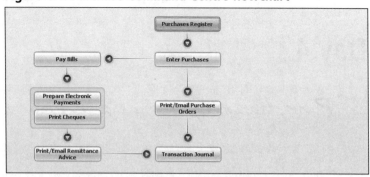

Business Basics, the introductory MYOB package, does not have a Purchase Command Centre, and many **microbusinesses** may avoid this area altogether, preferring to enter expenditure against Spend Money in the Banking Command Centre (which we discussed on day 2). It does take extra time to enter expenditure through the Purchase Command Centre, but the benefit of doing this is that it helps you to monitor and manage the business's cash flow and debts. As we noted towards the end of day 3, the Purchase Command Centre is a mirror image of the Sales Command Centre, so the screens and processes should feel familiar.

Purchases Linked Accounts

The Purchase Command Centre has its own specific Purchases Linked Accounts. To access these, go to Set-up → Linked Accounts → Purchase Accounts, and the Purchases Linked Accounts window will open (see figure 4.2). We discussed the concept of linked accounts on day 2 and again on day 3 in reference to the Banking and Sales Command Centre, so you should be feeling familiar with them. If you still find them confusing, it might be a good idea to arrange for an MYOB Certified Consultant to check that your linked accounts are set up correctly. Then leave them alone and forget about them!

Figure 4.2: Purchases Linked Accounts window

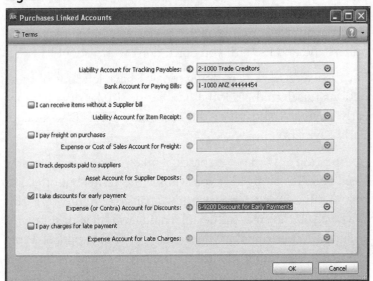

The first two lines relate to how accrual purchases are processed in MYOB. When a purchase is recorded through the Purchase Command Centre, the liability account Trade Creditors is used to record the amount payable. When the outstanding amount is paid against the purchase, the amount is transferred from the Trade Creditors account to the Bank account.

Purchase entered → Trade Creditors account → Bank account

If you wish to receive stock that has arrived with a delivery docket but no invoice, you need to check the first link, 'I can receive items without a Supplier bill'. Alternatively, this link can be set up when the need arises. As a purchase of this nature is processed, MYOB will alert the user to set up the linked account. The next four options are self-explanatory. Like 'I track deposits collected from customers', which we discussed on day 2 in reference to the Sales Command Centre, 'I track deposits paid to suppliers' can be fiddly, and I choose not to select this option.

In fact, many of my clients don't use any of these options and leave the links unchecked. If you pay freight on purchases, this feature will save you time and so it is worth taking the time to understand and use it. If you don't, don't worry about it.

For the exercises we are doing today, I have left four of these options unselected. Tick the box beside 'I take discounts for early payment' and select the account '5-9200 Discount for Early Payment'.

At the top of the Purchases Linked Accounts window (see figure 4.2 on p. 127) you will see the Terms button. Click this, and the Credit Terms window opens (see figure 4.3). This is where you can enter the default credit terms of your suppliers. In simple terms, when do you want to pay your suppliers? From your cash-flow point of view it's preferable, of course, for the payment terms to be as extended for as long as possible, but it's important to treat the relationship with respect and to pay in a timely manner.

Figure 4.3: Credit Terms window

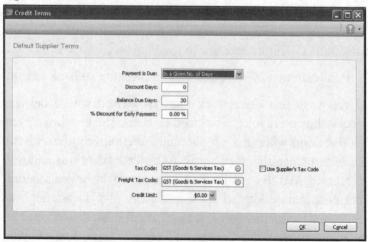

Change the terms as per the data in figure 4.3 to indicate that payment is due within 30 days of the invoice. All Suppliers you create *after* this change will reflect these credit terms. All Suppliers you created on day 1 will reflect the original default credit terms.

Purchase types: Quote, Order, Bill, Receive Item

There are four different purchase types in the Purchase Command Centre: Quote, Order, Bill and Receive Item. As in the Sales Command Centre, each type is clearly distinguished by colour: in this case, salmon pink for quotes, yellow for orders, pale powdery blue for bills and green for Receive Item. The Receive Item option is only available if an Item layout has been selected.

A Quote purchase type is simply a record in your system and has no further impact on anything. A quote can be converted to an order or a bill.

An Order purchase type does not create a transaction within MYOB unless it is an Item layout order. MYOB will then recognise that stock is on order and allow it to be sold through Sales. An order can be converted to a bill.

A Bill purchase type reflects the final supplier invoice.

Receive Items is a useful purchase type, as it recognises that stock has been received, usually with a delivery docket, and allows for it to be entered into the MYOB system and sold to a customer. When a bill is received, the Receive Item transaction can be converted to a bill and dollar amounts and additional details added.

Purchase layouts: Service, Item, Professional, Miscellaneous

MYOB provides four different purchase layouts: Service, Item, Professional and Miscellaneous. Unlike the Sales Command Centre, there is no Time Billing option. You can set the default purchase layout under Setup → Easy Setup Assistant → Purchases and allocate a default purchase layout to the individual Supplier Cards. When you are entering a purchase, you can change the layout by selecting the Layout button at the top of the Purchase window. Purchase layouts are used in a similar fashion to sales layouts in the Sales Command Centre.

▶ The Service layout is a standard all-purpose layout and can be used when the other options are not appropriate.

▶ The Item layout is used to record details of stock purchased. If items are inventoried, it's necessary to record the purchase through an Item layout so that it can be recorded as stock received and ready for a sale.

▶ The Professional layout is similar to the Service layout except that there is an additional column on the left-hand side where the date on which the service was provided can be entered.

▶ A Miscellaneous layout cannot be printed and can be used for adjusting purchases. Personally, I never use it.

Exercise 4.1

Go to the Purchase Command Centre, click the Enter Purchase button and spend some time exploring the different purchase types: Quote, Order, Bill and Receive Item, and the four purchase layouts: Service, Item, Professional and Miscellaneous.

Purchase Register and Transaction Journal

The Purchase Register (see figure 4.4) has six tabs across the top: All Purchases, Quotes, Orders, Open Bills, Returns and Debits, and Closed Bills. Depending on the tab selected, there are various buttons and information fields along the bottom. When using the Purchase Register, you can search by all suppliers or select just a single supplier in the Search By field. This can be very useful when you are reviewing your business's history with a supplier. (Figures 4.4 and 4.5, overleaf, are examples only; there will be no transactions in your data file.)

Figure 4.4: Purchase Register

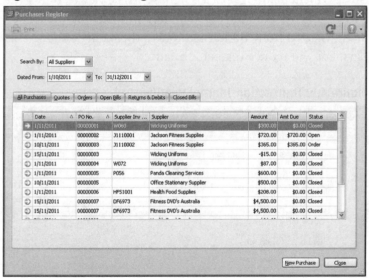

Note that if some transactions have been processed via Spend Money in the Banking Command Centre (which we covered on day 2), then the history you see here will not be complete. The Purchase Register can be used to create quotes and invoices, to convert quotes and orders to bills, and to pay bills.

Under the Returns and Debits tab, if a purchase is reversed, an adjustment note issued or overpayment is made, a refund can be received or applied to an existing purchase. If you are using an historical MYOB data file, check under the Returns and Debits tab to see if there are any historical transactions that you need to deal with.

The Purchases tab on the Transaction Journal window (see figure 4.5) details purchases in journal format. The purchase transaction credits the Trade Creditors account and debits either the Cost of Goods or Expense account and the GST Paid account.

Any payment made against a purchase can be viewed under the Disbursements tab, and this amount will then automatically be transferred from Trade Creditors to the Bank account. This payment will reduce the bank balance.

Figure 4.5: Transaction Journal window

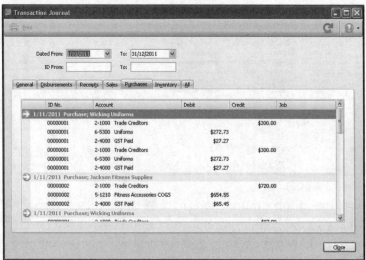

Entering purchases

The Purchase Command Centre is a valuable tool that can help you make business decisions and manage debt, but only if you enter transactions in a timely fashion.

Creating a Service quote

▶ Go to the Purchase Command Centre and click Enter Purchases, and the Purchases New Service window opens (see figure 4.6).

Figure 4.6: Purchases New Service window

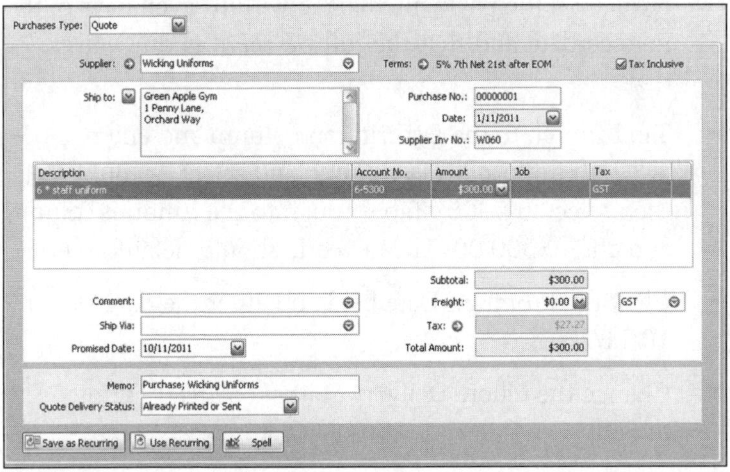

▶ Click the drop-down arrow in the Purchases Type field at top left and select Quote.

▶ Go to the Supplier field and enter 'Wicking Uniforms' as the Supplier, and then tab through this field. Once you have done this, the defaults set up in the Supplier Card will auto-fill out in the new purchase. All fields, however, can be overwritten.

- ▶ The purchase number is automatically generated.

- ▶ Click the Date field and enter the date 01/11/20XX.

- ▶ Click the zoom arrow beside Terms. Use the drop-down arrows to select the following options:

  - ⌀ Payment is Due: Day of Month after EOM

  - ⌀ Discount Date: 7th

  - ⌀ Balance Due: 21st

  - ⌀ % Discount for Early Payments: 5.00%

  These terms mean that a 5 per cent discount can be received if the payment is made within seven days of the invoice date and that the full payment is due within 21 days.

- ▶ Tab through to the Description column and enter '6 * staff uniform'. Tab through and select Account No., then select '6-5300'. Tab through to the Amount column and enter $300.00. The tax code should default to GST.

- ▶ Click the Promised Date field and enter the date 10/11/20XX.

- ▶ Change the Quote Delivery Status to Already Printed or Sent.

- ▶ Go to Menu Bar → Edit → Recap Transaction. An information window pops up and alerts you that 'There is no transaction to recap'. This is evidence that the purchase quote has not entered anything into MYOB. Click OK.

- ▶ Click the Send To button (at top left of the screen for AccountRight 20 and newer versions; at bottom right for older versions). MYOB will alert you that the quote will be saved. Click OK, click Email and then click Cancel.

▶ Click Cancel again to exit the window.

Creating a purchase order

▶ Go to the Purchase Command Centre and click the Purchases Register button. Then click the New Purchase button at bottom right. Enter Purchases, and the Purchases New Service Window opens (see figure 4.6 on p. 133).

▶ In the Purchase Type field select Order.

▶ Go to the Supplier field, click the drop-down arrow and select the New button at the bottom of the window. A new Supplier Card will be created.

▶ In the Name field enter 'Jackson Fitness Supplies'.

▶ Click the Buying Details tab. Use the drop-down arrows to select the following options:

    ¤   Purchase Layout: Service

    ¤   Expense Account: 5-1210 Fitness Accessories COGS

    ¤   Payment Memo: Yoga Mats

    ¤   Shipping Method: Courier

    ¤   Payment is Due: C.O.D.

    ¤   Credit Limit: $1000.00

    ¤   A.B.N. 56 565 656 565

▶ Click the Payment Details tab. Enter the following information:

    ¤   BSB Number: 454-454

¤   Bank Account Number: 4545454544

¤   Bank Account Name: Jackson Fitness Supplies

¤   Statement Text: Green Apple Gym

▶   Click OK to return to the Purchase Order window (see figure 4.7). If the Supplier field does not have 'Jackson Fitness Supplies', enter this. This saves you entry time, as several fields auto-fill from the Customer Card and the layout changes to Service.

Figure 4.7: Purchase Order window

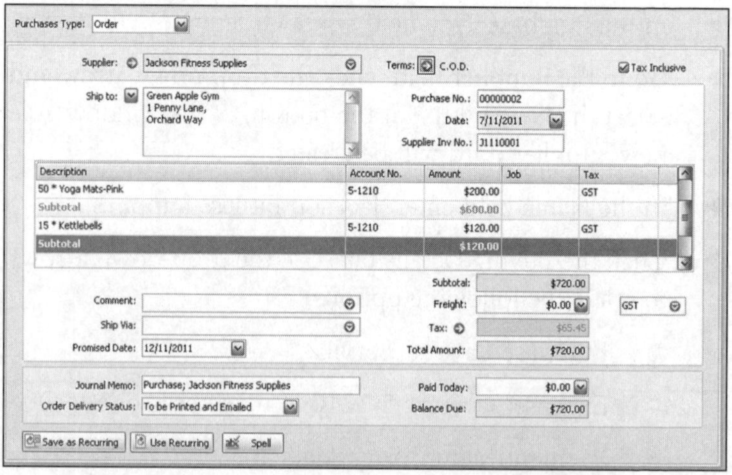

▶   Click the Date field and then press the space bar, and a calendar will pop up. Use the mouse to select '7 November 20XX'. Once you have selected a date, the calendar will close.

▶   Tab through to the Supplier Invoice No. field and enter 'J1110001', which is from the tax invoice Jackson Fitness Supplies issued the business.

▶ Tab through to enter details of the purchase. Right-click to bring up the context-sensitive menu (if this doesn't work, the trick is to do it when the row is highlighted blue) and select Insert Header, and then enter 'Yoga Mlats' in the Description column. (Yes, I know it has been spelt incorrectly—typos do happen in the real world; wait and see how we identify this one.) The line appears grey but will print out black. The text will not print out bold.

▶ Enter '50 * Yoga Mats-Blue' in the Description column.

▶ Tab through and '5-1210' should automatically appear from the card you created earlier. Tab through to the Amount column, enter $400, and the Tax fields should have auto-filled.

▶ Tab to the next line and enter '25 * Yoga Mats-Pink', then tab through and in the Amount column enter $200.

▶ Tab through to the next line, right-click to bring up the shortcut menu and select Insert Subtotal. A subtotal will be inserted in the Total column.

▶ Tab through to the next line and enter '15 * Kettlebells' and the amount $120.

▶ Tab through to the next line and insert a subtotal.

▶ Click the Promise Date field and enter 12/11/20XX.

▶ Click Order Delivery Status and select Already Printed or Sent.

▶ Click the Spelling button at bottom right. The system should recognise that 'Mlats' is an incorrect spelling. Choose the correct spelling, 'Mats', select Change and then click OK.

▶ Go to Menu Bar → Edit → Recap Transaction. An information window will pop up and alert you that 'There is no transaction to recap'. This is evidence that the purchase order has not entered anything into MYOB. Click OK.

▶ Click Record and then click Cancel to return to the Purchase Command Centre.

Exercise 4.2

Record the following purchase orders in a service layout:

▶ On 10 November Jackson Fitness Supplies confirmed an order for:

10 Fitballs at a cost of $12.50 each, total cost $125.00

40 Dumbbells at a cost of $4.00 each, total cost $160.00

10 Green Yoga Mats at a cost of $8.00 each, total cost $80.00

Jackson has now offered a 5 per cent discount if payment is made within five days of the invoice date, with payment due in 14 days. The purchase order number is J1110002.

When you start to create an order for Jackson Fitness Supplies, the Select From List window will open, giving you access to a previous order. Click Cancel, as you want to create a new purchase order.

▶ On 12 November Wicking Uniforms confirmed an additional order for two staff uniforms at $50.00 each. Wicking Uniforms' supplier invoice number is W072. Fill in the other information as you think best.

(Hint: Did you utilise headers and subtotals to create a neater invoice? Did you add any extra information?)

Entering a bill

The business can record the purchase as a tax deductible expense once you have been presented with the actual invoice for payment. Many bills will not need to be entered as quotes or orders; they can simply be entered as a bill. Likewise if the company does not have the actual invoice, you should not record the purchase as a bill, it should only be recognised as a Quote or an Order. When you receive an invoice from a supplier, it is important to check that it is accurate, that you have done business with this supplier, that you have received the goods or services detailed on the invoice, and that the invoice is added up accurately and has been properly authorised by someone within your business. There are always various scam invoices doing the rounds. For example, I have seen emails from what claim to be web domain companies asking for annual payment for your web domain and saying that if you don't pay you will lose your domain name. The scammers simply take the information from the internet and then try and fool unsuspecting people into paying them. I have also come across invoices with an incorrect total. It's always worth checking that you are indeed entering a legitimate bill.

▶ Go to the Purchase Command Centre, click Purchases Register at the top of the flow chart, and the Purchases Register opens. Click the All Purchases tab and click New Purchase at the bottom right of the Purchases Register and the Purchases Bill window will open (see figure 4.8, overleaf). The screen should be blue and it should say Purchases Type Bill in the top left-hand corner. If it says Quote or Order, click on the drop-down arrow and select Bill. As an alternative option, the Purchases Bill window could be reached by going to the Purchase Command Centre and clicking on Enter Purchases.

Figure 4.8: Purchase Bill window

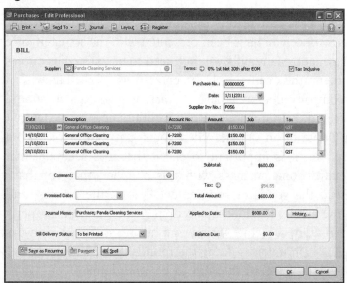

▶ Leave the Purchases Type as a Bill and select Panda Cleaning Services. If the layout does not automatically change, change it to Professional. Click OK.

▶ Enter the date as 1 November. Enter the supplier invoice number P056 and tab through to the box detailing what was purchased.

▶ In the Date column on the left, enter 7/10/XX. Enter General Office Cleaning in the Description column. Tab through and select '6-7200 Cleaning Expenses', and then tab through and enter $150 in the Amount column. The Professional layout allows you to include the date on which the service was provided. Replicate the weekly cleaning charge—that is, enter the information on 14, 21 and 28 October. The total of the bill should be $600. Notice a tax amount of $54.55.

▶ Click Record.

Exercise 4.3

Add additional information to the card for Office Stationery Supplies

Supplier: Office Stationery Supplies

Purchase Layout: Service

Expense Account: 6-1100 Office Stationery

Shipping Method: Courier

Payment is Due: C.O.D.

Credit Limit: $500.00

Converting a quote to a bill

▶ Go to the Purchases Command Centre and click Enter Purchases.

▶ In the Supplier field, type in Wicking Uniforms. Tab through, and the Select From List window opens. This provides a list of existing orders or quotes for the active supplier. Select Purchase Order 1 for $300 and click Use Purchase. The pink quote now appears. At the bottom of this screen select the Bill button (see figure 4.9, overleaf). The quote converts to a bill and the screen background changes to blue. All the terms remain the same. Go to Menu Bar → Edit → Recap Transactions, and note that there is now a journal entry and that this is a real transaction affecting Trade Creditors, GST and an expense account.

► Tab through to the Supplier Invoice No. field and enter W060 as the supplier invoice number.

► Click Record.

► At the Supplier field enter Jackson Fitness Supplies and tab through.

► Once again a Select From List window opens, with a list of existing orders and quotes for the supplier Jackson Fitness Supplies. Select the order dated 7 November 20XX and click Use Purchase.

► Change the date to 10/11/20XX. Go to the bottom and click the Bill button (see figure 4.9) to change the order to a bill.

► Click Record and then click Cancel.

Figure 4.9: Bill button

Once a quote or an order has been converted to a bill and recorded, it cannot be changed back to a quote or an order.

> **Turbo tip**
>
> If you received the sale in PDF format (perhaps from another MYOB user!), you can copy the description from the PDF and past it directly into the purchase, thus saving some time. Copy the description from the PDF, click in the Description column on the purchase, right-click to bring up the context-sensitive menu, and select Paste.

Paying bills

There are several ways you can process the payment of bills in MYOB: through the Pay Bills window, by electronic batching, or by using the To Do List from the Command Panel. It's important that purchases entered via the Purchase Command Centre be paid through the Purchase Command Centre and not through the Spend Money option in the Banking Command Centre (as we covered on day 2).

The Pay Bills area records payments against orders and bills; it does not record payments against quotes.

Paying bills by cheque

▶ Go to the Purchase Command Centre and click the Pay Bills button, and the Pay Bills Window opens (see figure 4.10).

Figure 4.10: Pay Bills window

Purchase No.	Status		Date	Amount	Discount	Total Owed	Amount Applied
00000004	Open	↻	12/11/2011	$100.00	$0.00	$100.00	$0.00
00000001	Open	→	10/11/2011	$300.00	$15.00	$285.00	$285.00

Supplier: Wicking Uniforms

Payee: Wicking Uniforms

Two Hundred and Eighty Five Dollars and 0 Cents

Memo: Payment; Wicking Uniforms

Cheque No.: 2

Date: 15/11/2011

Amount: $285.00

Green Apple Gym

☐ Include Closed Purchases

☑ Cheque Already Printed

Remittance Advice Delivery Status: To be Printed

Total Applied:	$285.00
Finance Charge:	$0.00
Total Paid:	$285.00
Out of Balance:	$0.00

▶ At the top of the screen you can choose the account from which the money will be paid. It will either be paid from the cheque account or be grouped with electronic payments. The latter is similar to the Spend Money window in the Banking Command Centre (which we discussed on day 2). For these exercises the payments will come out of 1-1000 ANZ 44444454 unless stated otherwise.

▶ Click the Supplier field and then the drop-down arrow, and you will see an alphabetical list of suppliers and the current balances owed to them. Click Wicking Uniforms, and the Pay Bills window auto-fills with open bills linked to this supplier.

▶ At top right you will see an option to enter a cheque or reference number. As we discussed on day 2 in reference to the Banking Command Centre, the other options are CASH, VISA, BS (Bank Statement), PAY, BPAY and EFT. Leave the cheque number that is automatically generated.

▶ Tab through to the Date field and enter 15 November 20XX. Tab through to the Amount field and enter $285.00. The original invoice was for $300, but Wicking Uniforms offers a 5 per cent discount if it is paid within seven days. MYOB recognises that the payment will be within the seven-day period and calculates a discount of $15. (If you do not see a discount, have you entered all the dates correctly?)

▶ You *must* enter the total amount applied in the Amount Applied column. If you don't properly apply an amount in this column, the total amount may inadvertently insert itself in the Finance Charges field at bottom right of the Pay Bills window. I have come across clients who were unaware that they were doing this, and it is quite a fiddly and time-consuming process to correct this mistake. Apply the payment amount carefully against the open bill.

▶ A $15 discount has been awarded for this prompt payment.

▶ Press Ctrl + R at the same time, and the Recap Transactions window opens. The transaction has created three journal entries. The first reflects the payment of $285 being made from the Bank account, which reduces the Trade Creditors account.

▶ The next two journal entries are somewhat complicated, reflecting how MYOB treats the $15 discount. Trade Creditors is reduced, and the Cost of Goods line reflects a discount for early payment of $13.64 (not $15, as this amount includes a GST component). You don't normally need to worry about the journal entry, or the treatment of the discount; it should work itself out. However, if for some reason you had to delete the payment and reprocess it, it would be necessary to delete the journals related to the discount as well.

▶ The Remittance Advice Delivery Status field will show the default option 'To be Printed'.

▶ When you click Record, a window will pop up advising you that the payment includes one discount and will result in one debit memo. In simple terms, MYOB is processing the discount and allocating it to the original cost or expense, thus reducing the cost or expense, as we discussed earlier.

Paying bills electronically

▶ Go to the Purchase Command Centre and click the Purchase Register.

▶ Click the Open Bills tab, click the line for Panda Cleaning Services, and then click the Pay Bill button at bottom left, and the Pay Bills window opens (see figure 4.10 on p. 143).

▶ At the top, select 'Group with electronic payments'. Enter EFT in the Cheque No. field.

▶ The amount applied is $600. Edit the memo to include a reference to the month of October.

▶ Click Record and then click Close.

Exercise 4.4

1 Convert the Wicking Uniforms order into a bill and process a payment against it using a cheque dated 15/11/XX. Remember to change the account from which the payment will be made to '1-1000 ANZ 44444454', before recording the transaction.

2 Enter a bill for Office Stationery Supplier for $500, dated 12/11/XX. Pay the Office Stationery Supplier bill electronically on 15/11/XX.

Preparing electronic payments

On day 2 we worked through the procedure for setting up electronic payments in the Banking Command Centre. You need to set up the bank account details of the payment bank account and to enter the payment details of the supplier.

▶ Go to the Purchase Command Centre and click the Prepare Electronic Payments button on the left-hand side, and the Prepare Electronic Payments window will open (see figure 4.11).

Figure 4.11: Prepare Electronic Payments window

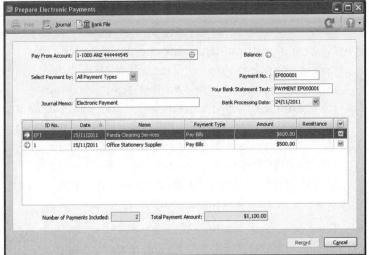

▶ The Pay From Account field is linked to the bank account from which the payment will be made. On the same line on the right-hand side, the Balance field shows the current balance of the bank account. If you click the zoom arrow beside the word Balance, you will go to the Find Transaction window, with the Cheque Account field active. If necessary you can review transactions against this account here, but for our present purposes click the Close button.

▶ Change the date to 24/11/XX.

▶ Click the drop-down arrow beside the 'Select Payment by' field. Select Spend Money and the list of open payments due in the centre box will disappear, because there are no electronic payments to be made against a Spend Money transaction. Go back and click the drop-down arrow and select the Pay Bills option and the open payments will reappear, because they are Pay Bills payment types.

▶ Now go to the right-hand side and tick the check box on the centre box title row. This will select all listed open payments. Note the two Total fields at bottom right: Number of Payments Included and Total Payment Amount. These are useful for double-checking the electronic payment that is about to be made. If the current MYOB balance shown at top right is accurate, checking this against the total payment that is to be made will ensure that you have sufficient funds available.

▶ For the purpose of this exercise we are creating a bank file, so click the Bank File button at the top of the screen (or the bottom of the screen for older versions of MYOB). The transaction will be recorded and a bank file will be created. However, the banking information is incomplete and we need to enter it to complete the transaction.

▶ When the Information window opens, click OK. You need to obtain electronic banking information from your own bank. Use the following data to complete the bank account set-up:

   ¤ Electronic Payment Type: check the box 'I create Bank Files'.

⋈   Bank Code: ANZ

⋈   Direct Entry User ID: 100

▶   Try to click Bank File again, and you will be alerted to further incomplete information: the Supplier Cards' banking information is required.

▶   When the Supplier Cards were originally created, the suppliers' bank account details were not entered on their cards. Use the following data for the bank details of the two suppliers:

⋈   BSB Number: 111-111

⋈   Bank Account Number: 111111111

⋈   Bank Account Name: Panda Cleaning Services

⋈   Statement Text: Green Apple Gym

⋈   BSB Number: 111-222

⋈   Bank Account Number: 222222222

⋈   Bank Account Name: Office Stationery Supplier

⋈   Statement Text: Green Apple Gym

▶   When you have entered the data, the Save As window will pop up. I usually like to save the file [ANZ.ABA] to my desktop, as the file created is not something I need to keep for the long term.

▶   You now need to upload the bank file that has been created to your online bank facility. As we discussed on day 2 in reference to the Banking Command Centre, the bank should provide you with security codes and explain how to do this.

Printing cheques

MYOB can be set up to print cheques. In all my years of using MYOB I have come across only one person who uses this facility. If you still use cheques, however, it's a timesaving option.

You can purchase professional-quality, personalised business cheque paper from MYOB, which has a relationship with Forms Express. The business stationery saves you the time you would otherwise spend writing cheques and includes a remittance section.

▶ To print cheques from MYOB, go to the Purchase Command Centre and click the Print Cheques button, and the Review Cheques Before Printing window opens.

▶ Click F1 [Function-1] on your keyboard and the Help Centre will open in a new window, with specific Help topics for printing cheques. Take some time to read the information, and click any other topics that may be of interest to you. It's useful to remember that F1 can be used on many screens to access information relevant to the specific area you are working in.

▶ Go back to your MYOB software and click Advanced Filters on the right-hand side, and the Advanced Filters window opens (see figure 4.12). Here you can select the bank account from which the cheque will be paid and enter the next cheque number. There are filters to select the cheques to be printed, and you can select a customised cheque form.

Figure 4.12: Advanced Filters window

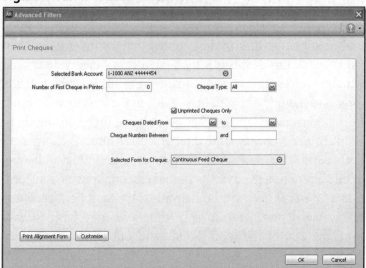

▶ At bottom left you will see the Print Alignment Form button, which allows you to do a test run to ensure that the printer has aligned with the pre-printed cheque form. The Customise button provides access to customising the active cheque form in the 'Selected Form for Cheque' field.

▶ Click the OK button and tick the check box on the far left-hand side to select the cheque to be printed. Click the Print button, and the Print window opens. Check the settings and select Print again.

Exercise 4.5

Print the cheques for Wicking Uniforms (see exercise 4.2 on p. 138).

Printing/emailing a remittance advice

A remittance advice is simply a document the customer sends to the supplier to inform the supplier that the invoice has been paid. It contains details of which payments were made against which invoices. If you were to pay your bills by cheques, it is typical to include a remittance advice in the envelope. Though I discourage payments by cheque, they are time consuming to produce and process, and the bank may impose charges on both parties for paying by cheque and receipting a cheque. While a remittance advice is not an essential business record, it is a courtesy and will be helpful to the supplier's accounts receivable department. To save time you may wish to wait until the end of the month and send out all the remittance advices in one batch.

Some of the MYOB invoice templates that come with the software include a cut-off section at the base of the invoice that is designed for use as a remittance advice slip. There are also standalone remittance advice slips, which can be customised. When you customise your remittance advice slips take the opportunity to promote your business to your supplier by adding details of the services your business offers.

▶   Go to the Purchase Command Centre. Take a few moments to look at the flow chart in the centre of the screen that shows the flow of the processes in the Purchase Command Centre. The Purchase is entered and the bill is paid electronically or by cheque. The next step in the process is to click the Print/Email Remittance Advice button and the Review Remittance Advices Before Delivery window opens (see figure 4.13).

Figure 4.13: Review Remittance Advices Before Delivery window

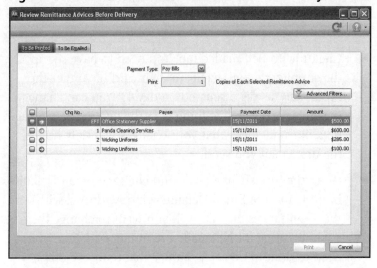

▶ At top left there are two tabs: To Be Printed and To Be Emailed. When we discussed paying a bill, you will recall that there was a field at bottom left of the Pay Bills screen entitled Remittance Advice Delivery Status, with four options to choose from:

    ⌀ To Be Printed

    ⌀ To Be Emailed

    ⌀ To Be Printed and Emailed

    ⌀ Already Printed or Sent.

▶ The remittance advice feeds into the Review Remittance Advice Before Delivery window, depending on the selection made in the Pay Bills screen. That may all sound rather complicated, but essentially, if you want to email a remittance advice you need to select the To Be Emailed option in the Remittance Advice Delivery Status window. But if you didn't do this, don't fret—the

Advanced Filters button will allow you to access payments that were not assigned the desired delivery status.

▶ Click the To Be Emailed tab. You need to have set up the supplier's email details in their card file under the Profile tab (as we discussed on day 1). You can change the email message by typing over the text in the Message box, but remember that your changes will only hold for the first email you send.

▶ Go to the top left-hand side and click the Email Defaults button, and the Email Defaults window opens, with the Remittances tab active. If you want to change the email message for all emailed remittance advices, you need to do it in this area. Notice that there are other tabs accessing email messages relevant to different areas: Sales, Purchases, Statements, Remittances and Pay Slips.

▶ Click OK and then click Cancel.

Exercise 4.6

Email a remittance advice to yourself by changing the email address to your own email address. When you receive the email, take a close look at the message and the attachment.

Printing and emailing purchase orders

A purchase order is a legal document issued to a supplier detailing the goods and services that the customer wishes to procure. It's good practice for a supplier to deliver goods and services only when an authorised purchase order is in place. You will recall that on day 3 we entered the Customer Purchase Order on the Sales Invoice. This indicated that the business was supplying goods or services against an authorised purchase order. The Purchase Orders window is very similar to the Remittance Advice Window. In this window you can access purchase orders, select forms, edit email defaults, and print or email purchase orders.

Purchases reconciliation

Purchases reconciliation is essentially the process of checking what has been processed in the Purchase Command Centre against the Trade Creditors account to see if they match. To check that everything is in order, you can review the Payables Reconciliation Exceptions Report.

▶ Go to the Accounts Command Centre and click the Company Data Auditor button on the right-hand side. We discussed the Company Data Auditor briefly on day 1 in reference to the Accounts Command and Card File Centres. It is tool for reviewing the integrity of data in many different areas of MYOB. In this activity we are using it to highlight any potential issues with the purchases reconciliation.

▶ Click the Next button twice, and the Transaction Review tab is highlighted.

▶ Change the Start Date to 1 July 20XX and the End Date to 25 November 20XX, and then click the button Run Review. The second line, 'Reconcile purchases with linked payables accounts', is essentially a purchase reconciliation for the period reviewed. If a question mark appears, click the Display button, and the Payables Reconciliation Exceptions Report is displayed, highlighting potential issues. If there are issues, revise the date range to an earlier date when the Purchases Receivables matched the Trade Creditors account, and then move forward day by day to discover the date at which they no longer matched. Review and correct the transactions on that date. Typically, the error is a posting made directly to the Trade Creditors account. If you have entered the transaction from this book correctly, the Display button option will not appear at the Payables Reconciliation Exceptions Report line.

Analysing payables

There are a variety of reports in MYOB that display payables. Go to the Purchases Command Centre and click the Business Insights button at bottom right of the Command Panel to see various reports about your suppliers. Another area where you can analyse payables is under Reports → Purchases → Payables. Here you will find various Aged Payables reports. As we discussed previously, the total amount listed in the Analyse Payables window (see figure 4.14) should equal the Trade Creditors account balance.

Figure 4.14: Analyse Payables [Summary] extract

				Green Apple Gym	
Aged Payables [Summary]				1 Penny Lane, Orchard Way	
As of 31/10/2011				ABN: 44 554 455 445	
				Email: green@applegym.com	
Name	**Total Due**	**0 - 30**	**31 - 60**	**61 - 90**	**90+**
Australia Post	$50.00	$50.00	$0.00	$0.00	$0.00
Jackson Fitness Supplies	$1,085.00	$1,085.00	$0.00	$0.00	$0.00
Total:	$1,135.00	$1,135.00	$0.00	$0.00	$0.00
Ageing Percent:		100.0%	0.0%	0.0%	0.0%

The ageing criteria can be changed under Setup → Preferences, as we discussed on day 1. The zoom arrows drill down to detailed purchases information. As with all reports, it's important when using this window to check that the financial information is up-to-date and that all receipts have been applied to the invoices. You can access detailed and summarised Aged Payables reports via the Reports menu on the Control Panel, and you can customise these reports to show the payments due from individual, selected or all suppliers.

In order to survive in business and maintain a positive cash flow, you need to minimise expenditure. Using the Purchase Command Centre effectively will enable you to keep your business expenses under control.

Plan your expenditure

When considering any business expenditure, ask yourself whether it's really necessary, and if so, whether you need it *now*? Will you utilise the item or service as soon as it's purchased or can the expenditure be delayed?

This is an example of why it's useful to have a budget in place for your business. If you have already determined your spending limits for the year or quarter, it will be much easier to decide whether a particular expense is warranted.

MYOB has the ability to create a budget for the current and next financial year, and also to produce multi-period budget spreadsheets.

▶ Go to the Account Command Centre and click the Accounts List, and then go to the Expenses tab and double-click Postage Expense.

▶ Click the Budgets button at top left, and the Prepare Budgets window opens. Expenses can be allocated to different months, either individually or by using the Shortcuts button.

▶ Enter $200 in the July column alongside Telephone Expenses, and click Copy Amount to Following Months. Select OK.

▶ Now go and look at the Report. Click Reports → Accounts → Profit and Loss [Budget Analysis] → Display, and the Report displayed shows a comparison between actuals and budgeted figures.

Using budgets within MYOB will help you to plan your business expenditure. If you find the prospect of putting together a complete budget for your business too daunting, at least formulate a plan and a time frame for expenditure on major areas of your business.

Assess the return on your investment

What is the return on investment (ROI) of the expenditure? The ROI is defined as profit of investment divided by cost of investment, and so the higher the figure, the more lucrative the investment. What will the investment return to the business over a period of time—say, over a year? Will it help to generate income? Will it have a resale value? Do you really understand what it will contribute to the business?

With the answers to all these questions in mind, is it worth the money?

The ROI of some types of investments can be tracked using the Job function in MYOB. It is a relatively easy concept to understand and use. Let's look at an example I use in my own business to demonstrate what I mean.

I offer secure remote MYOB support through a service called GoToAssist. I set up a Job called 'GoToAssist' via Menu Bar → Lists → Jobs → New. I allocate the job code 'GoToAssist' against this monthly cost when I process the transaction. I also allocate the job code 'GoToAssist' to sales invoices for clients who use this service. I am now tracking both the income generated from using the service and the cost of providing the service, and thus I can calculate the profit. I have all the information required to calculate the ROI. This information will help me to decide whether or not to continue offering the service.

Comparison shop

If you decide to go ahead with the expenditure, shop around, compare prices, seek quotes, watch the sales, use vouchers and always try to negotiate a better price.

Be accountable for your business spending

As a soloist, are you holding yourself accountable for your spending? Discussing your business expenditure with your partner, accountant, business coach or advisory board on a regular basis can be a valuable business growth strategy, and may help you to identify new ways to save money

Think outside the box

Is there a way you can have the product or service you want without spending the money? Are borrowing, co-sharing or renting options available?

Like one of my clever clients, you may find it fun to turn money-saving into a game, competing against yourself to spend less and less with every passing month. Another of my clients rents an office for his business and sublets the space he doesn't need at a rate that more than covers his own rent.

It may seem exhausting and onerous to apply these expense management guidelines to every purchase, but it's crucial to understand that unnecessary expenditure could lead to cash flow problems. I have firsthand experience of seeing businesses misguidedly outlay huge expenses early in their operation, only to teeter on the brink of collapse for months or years afterwards. By spending money wisely will help your business to achieve stability and longevity.

Summary of day 4

Day 4 has introduced you to the Purchase Command Centre: how it is set up, how purchases are processed, how bills are paid, and how MYOB software can be used to manage debt payments. Understanding this area and using it efficiently will contribute directly to a healthy profit and cash flow.

On day 5 we will explore the Inventory Command Centre, which offers a simple stock-management function for a small business. Some businesses may never need to monitor stock, so if that applies to your business you can have tomorrow off and go to the gym! Other businesses start off using the MYOB Inventory Command Centre but discover that their stock systems are too complicated for a basic AccountRight MYOB package and that they need to upgrade to an MYOB ERP solution such as Exo Business. Details of the available software can be found on the MYOB website.

Day 5

Inventory Command Centre

Key terms and concepts

▶ *Stock:* the items a trading business buys and sells; for example, the stock of a paint store would include cans of paint cans and rollers.

▶ *Inventory:* a listing of items or stock the businesses purchases and sells.

Introduction and overview

Day 5 introduces you to the Inventory Command Centre (see figure 5.1, overleaf). In this area you can create inventory items, set prices, adjust or count inventory levels, and combine inventory through the auto-build processes. The MYOB package AccountRight is a basic inventory management solution. Even if you don't use inventory, it's worth understanding what can and can't be done here, to see if it will benefit your record-keeping system.

Figure 5.1: Inventory Command Centre flowchart

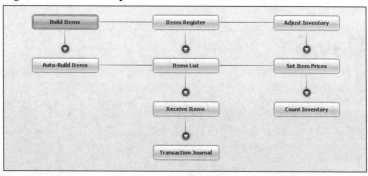

Some businesses try to use MYOB AccountRight software to manage business processes the program was never meant to manage. So a word to the wise: don't get too ambitious, and take the time to understand the system's limitations. If you have what could be classified as a retail store, or your business requires the use of a till, consider using MYOB Retail Basics or MYOB Retail Manager, as their functionality is more suited to that environment. There is a network of Retail Manager professionals who can assist you with any Retail Manager queries you have. It's worth mentioning that MYOB AccountRight Enterprise supports multiple warehousing and negative stock, whereas the smaller AccountRight packages do not have this capability.

Periodic and perpetual inventory

Before we start exploring the Inventory Command Centre or setting up our inventory system, we need to understand the difference between the concepts of periodic and perpetual inventory within MYOB AccountRight. You will then be able to judge which is better suited to your business.

Essentially, a periodic inventory system does not count inventory coming in or leaving the business. It relies on a stocktake undertaken at the end of the year. The value of the Asset account Inventory and the Cost of Inventory Sold account are updated as a result of a stocktake. The Income account recognises income as the inventory is sold.

A perpetual inventory system undertakes continuous counts of the inventory within the business. It does this by recognising the inventory purchased and sold and any adjustments that are made as these things occur. The Asset account Inventory should reflect the inventory on hand, and the Cost of Sale account reflects the sale of the item and is updated accordingly. In MYOB this is done through the use of linked accounts, which we will be discussing in this section.

Table 5.1 outlines the effect that inventory transactions have on the accounts in perpetual and periodic inventory systems. You may find it useful to refer back to this table as you process the transactions we cover in this section. In MYOB AccountRight the concepts of periodic and perpetual inventory are slightly simplified compared to the rules that apply to these concepts in some other MYOB packages.

Table 5.1: effect of inventory transactions on the accounts in perpetual and periodic inventory systems

Perpetual inventory				
	Recording of delivery of goods	Entering an inventory purchase	Entering an inventory sale	Stocktake
Profit and loss				
Income	-	-	✓	✓
Cost of sales	-	-	✓	✓

Table 5.1: *(cont'd)*

Perpetual inventory *(cont'd)*				
	Recording of delivery of goods	Entering an inventory purchase	Entering an inventory sale	Stocktake
Balance sheet				
Inventory	-	✓	✓	✓
Stock number	✓			
Periodic inventory				
	Recording of delivery of goods	Entering an inventory purchase	Entering an inventory sale	Stocktake
Profit and loss				
Income	-	-	✓	✓
Cost of sales	-	✓	-	✓
Balance sheet				
Inventory	-	-	-	✓
Stock number				

In MYOB, inventory is held as 'Items', so the first thing we need to look at is how we go about creating an Item. Personally, I find this terminology a little odd and prefer the word stock, but it's obviously important to understand how this term is used in MYOB. The following exercise takes you through the process of creating a stock item.

Exercise 5.1

To do the exercise, we shall need to add and edit some general ledger account codes. First edit the account number '1-4000 Payroll Clearing' to '1-1510' and then create the general ledger accounts shown in table 5.2.

Table 5.2: general ledger accounts

Account number	Account name	Type	Tax code	Header/ detail
1-1400	INVENTORY	Assets		H
1-1410	Equipment Inventory	Other Current Assets	N-T	D
1-1420	Health Food Inventory	Other Current Assets	N-T	D
1-1430	DVD Inventory	Other Current Assets	N-T	D
4-1400	INVENTORY INCOME	Income		H
4-1410	Equipment Income	Income	GST	D
4-1420	Health Food Income	Income	GST	D
4-1430	DVD Income	Income	GST	D
5-1400	INVENTORY COGS	COS		H
5-1410	Equipment COGS	COS	GST	D
5-1420	Health Food COGS	COS	GST	D
5-1430	DVD COGS	COS	GST	D
5-2000	Stock Write-Offs	COS	GST	D

You will also need to create two new suppliers, Fitness DVDs Australia and Health Food Supplies, both with an Item purchase layout.

Creating an Item

To create a new Item, click the Inventory Command Centre, click the Item List and then click New, and the Items Profile window opens (see figure 5.2, overleaf). Across the top of the window you should see six tabs: Profile, Item Details, Buying Details, Selling Details, History and Auto-Build. The MYOB

AccountRight Enterprise package has an additional tab, Locations (not shown here).

Figure 5.2: Items Profile window

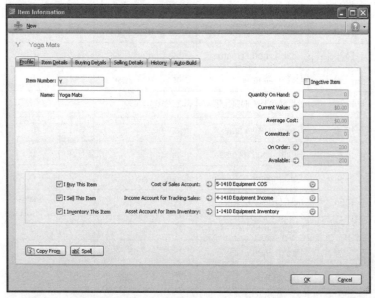

The first two fields in this window are Item Number and Name. Before you launch into creating your inventory, it's a good idea to give some thought to a consistent naming convention.

Inventory naming and numbering conventions

There are various issues you need to consider when naming inventory. When you search for inventory within MYOB, all Items with text matching the search terms will be displayed in the Items List, so it's worth setting up a system to distinguish each Item. For example, it can be useful to add a simple code to the Item Number—such as AU, US or CA to indicate the source country—along with any other brief reference that will identify the Item for you. If your supplier network is simple and you source your products from single suppliers, it makes sense to use the supplier number as the Item Number.

If you precede the Item Number with a backward slash, the number will not appear on the printed sale or purchase; only the description will appear. This is useful when you want to add comments.

On the right-hand side of the Items Profile window (see figure 5.2) you will see a snapshot of information about the items with a zoom arrow beside each field. This allows you to drill down and review detailed information. The Quantity on Hand (QOH) reflects the stock in the business storerooms, irrespective of whether there is stock on hand or stock committed. The Current Value is the GST-exclusive dollar value of the stock in the storerooms. The Average Cost is a calculation of Current Value divided by QOH. 'Committed' is a reflection of Sales Orders, and On Order is a reflection of Purchase Orders. The number in the Available field is QOH plus stock On Order less stock Committed, and is thus dependent on both supplier and customer deliveries.

In the centre area of the Items Profile window you can see the linked account options 'I buy', 'I sell' and 'I inventory'. These enable you to set up the Item in the appropriate way. For instance, a packaging product such as bubble wrap could simply be linked to 'I buy', while a DVD would be linked to 'I buy' and 'I sell'. You will recall from day 2 that linked accounts allow information to flow to the correct area behind the scenes.

If you opt to use a perpetual inventory system, the majority of your items will be linked to 'I inventory'. Items in a periodic inventory system, however, would not be linked to 'I inventory'.

Many businesses will have a mixture of perpetual and periodic items, depending on the complexity of their management and reporting requirements.

If you are setting up inventory in MYOB software, it's worth considering whether the inventory can be grouped and whether this will be an aid to decision making. The Items List area does not allow for headers, unlike the Jobs or the General Ledger accounts areas. Grouping gets around this. Obviously, grouping the inventory will also give you a clearer idea of stock levels, income, cost of sales and gross profit at the level of subsets.

You need to give careful thought to how best you can group items within your own business, so you will most likely want to come back to this. I would suggest a minimum of three and, in most cases, a maximum of 10 groups. If you have more than 10 groups, you need to ask yourself whether MYOB AccountRight is the right software for your business. Using the Green Apple Gym as an example, inventory could be split into three groups: Equipment, DVDs and Health Food, as shown in figure 5.3.

Figure 5.3: inventory chart of accounts

	Inventory	Income	Cost of sales
Equipment	1-1410 Equipment Inventory	4-1410 Equipment Income	5-1410 Equipment COS
Health Food	1-1420 Health Food Inventory	4-1420 Health Food Income	5-1420 Health Food COS
DVD	1-1430 DVD Inventory	4-1430 DVD Income	5-1430 DVD COS

There may be 50 different items that fall under the Equipment category. They can be viewed individually, but if you set up the chart of accounts as shown in figure 5.3 they can be subtotalled and viewed as a group. To see the effect of this, go to the Chart of Accounts and click the Inventory Assets tab, and the Accounts List: Asset Inventory groups window opens (see figure 5.4). The header account '1-1400 INVENTORY' is the total value of inventory on hand, and the three accounts below, Equipment, Health Food and DVD, represent the groups of inventory. You can view details of individual inventory items in a number of areas, so it's not appropriate to detail each item individually in the chart of accounts. (Figures 5.4, 5.5 and 5.6, overleaf, are examples only; there will be no transactions in your data file.)

Figure 5.4: Accounts List: Asset Inventory groups

	Account Number	Account Name	Type	Tax Code	Linked	Balance
⊙	1-1400	INVENTORY	Asset			$8,339.00
⊙	1-1410	Equipment Inventory	Other Asset	N-T		$0.00
⊙	1-1420	Health Food Inventory	Other Asset	N-T		$157.18
⊙	1-1430	DVD Inventory	Other Asset	N-T		$8,181.82

In the Income Inventory groups (see figure 5.5), the detailed groups can be seen in the Income area. The header account '4-1400 INVENTORY INCOME' is the total value of income from inventory sales. This is split across Equipment, Health Food and DVD Inventory.

Figure 5.5: Accounts List: Income Inventory groups

	Account Number	Account Name	Type	Tax Code	Linked	Balance
➔	4-0000	Income	Income			$875.36
⊙	4-1210	Fitness Accessories Sales	Income	GST		$0.00
⊙	4-1400	INVENTORY INCOME	Income			$39.00
⊙	4-1410	Equipment Income	Income	GST		$33.00
⊙	4-1420	Health Food Income	Income	GST		$6.00
⊙	4-1430	DVD Income	Income	GST		$0.00

Finally, in the Cost of Sales Inventory groups (figure 5.6, overleaf) the header account '5-1400 INVENTORY COS' is the total cost of inventory, and the three account groups are detailed below this. After you have worked with MYOB for a while you will recognise that the prefix '5' refers to Cost of Sales, and that the prefix '4' refers to Income, and so on.

Figure 5.6: Cost of Sales Inventory groups

	Account Number	Account Name	Type	Tax Code	Linked	Balance
→	5-0000	Cost Of Sales	Cost of Sales			$12,726.07
↺	5-1100	Fitness Equipment COGS	Cost of Sales	GST		$0.00
↺	5-1210	Fitness Accessories COGS	Cost of Sales	GST		$654.55
↺	5-1400	INVENTORY COS	Cost of Sales			$70.60
↺	5-1410	Equipment COS	Cost of Sales	GST		$68.18
↺	5-1420	Health Food COS	Cost of Sales	GST		$2.42
↺	5-1430	DVD COS	Cost of Sales	GST		$0.00

How does all this affect the Inventory report? If you look at the Profit and Loss Statement at Level 2, only the total Inventory, Income and Inventory Cost of Sale account headers are displayed. Drilling down further to Level 3 reveals the detail. Detailed information about each inventory Item can be found under the Item List tab.

The Item Details window (see figure 5.7) allows you record information about the item. A space for an image is provided, but the image is saved outside the MYOB data file and so does not increase the size of the data file. The Description field is an expanded field where you can add further information about the item. As you would expect, if you check the box Use Item Description on Sales and Purchases, the information appears on both invoices and bills, in an editable format. There are six customisable fields available, similar to those we explored when we discussed Customer and Supplier Cards on day 1.

In the Item Information: Buying Details window (see figure 5.8) the Last Purchase Price is a non-editable field and reflects the last purchase transaction.

Figure 5.7: Item Information: Item Details window

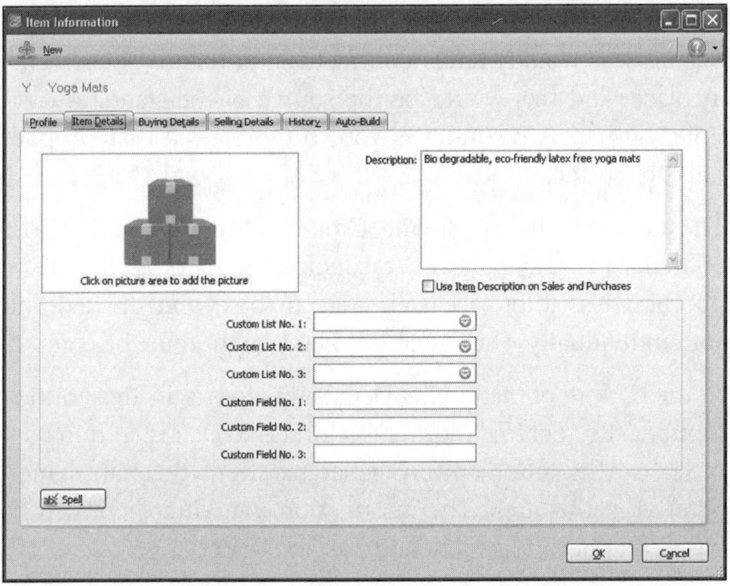

Figure 5.8: Item Information: Buying Details window

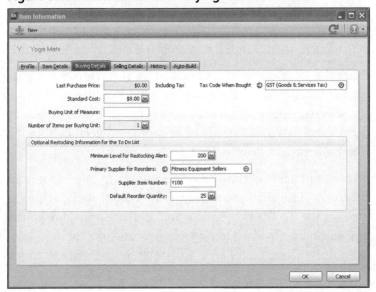

The Standard Cost can be entered here, and when a purchase is created the standard cost will auto-fill from this field. Some businesses would have contractual purchase agreements in place, and this would be the source of the standard cost. Entering it here also allows you to crosscheck that supplier bills are correct.

The next two fields, Buying Unit of Measure and Number of Items per Buying Unit, recognise that a product can be purchased as a lot (a barrel, crate or box) and divided and sold individually. The tax code when bought must be entered.

At the bottom of the Buying Details window is an area entitled Optional Restocking Information for the To Do List. A purchase order can be automatically generated from the information entered in this area. The information you enter here will be based on your judgement and past experience.

The stock level you enter in the Minimum Level for Restocking Alert field should take into consideration how long it takes for orders to be delivered by the supplier concerned and how fast the business moves stock. The dwindling stock level needs to be sufficient to last until a new stock order arrives.

Enter the usual supplier for the item in the Primary Supplier for Reorders field. In the Supplier Item Number field, enter the selected primary supplier's item number for the item. The quantity of items that needs to be reordered is entered in the Default Reorder Quantity field.

To see the results of the Optional Restocking Information for the To Do List area, you will need to look at the Stock Alert area on the To Do List. Escape out to the Command Centre and click the To Do List, which is found on the left-hand side of the Command Panel. Click the Stock Alert tab to see a list of stock that has dropped below the minimum level for restocking. From this area you can create a purchase order based on the information from the Item Information: Buying Details window (see figure 5.8 on p. 171). We will discuss the To Do List and the Stock Alert tab further on day 7.

The Item Information: Selling Details window (see figure 5.9) includes an editable field called Base Selling Price. The Selling Unit of Measure (for example, each, litres or centimetres) can be entered here and will be shown on the invoice. The Number of Items per Selling Unit field allows for selling in batches and possibly offering a bulk discount. The tax code when sold must be entered. The centre field seen here is a pricing option matrix that is only available in MYOB AccountRight Premier, and is suited to businesses with complex pricing structures.

Figure 5.9: Item Information: Selling Details window

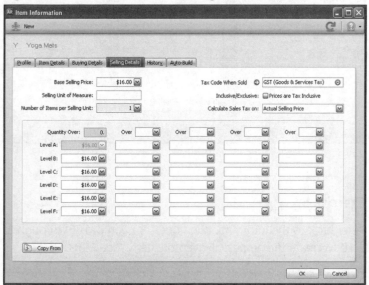

The Item Information: History window (see figure 5.10) is a snapshot of the unit and dollar value of monthly sales, the cost of sales, and purchases. In this window the columns are moveable. Hover over the header row, left-click and drag, and the arrows in the top right-hand corner can switch between different financial years. Remember that, as in most areas of MYOB, the dollar values are GST-exclusive.

Figure 5.10: Item Information: History window

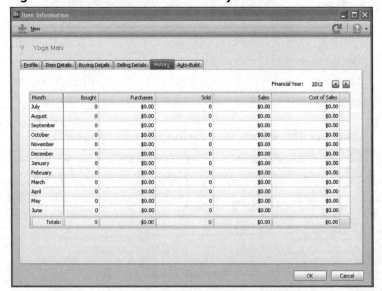

Exercise 5.2

Refer back to the information in figures 5.2 (on p. 166) through to 5.10 to create the perpetual inventory item Yoga Mats.

Exercise 5.3

Create the periodic inventory item Zumba Shakers from the data in table 5.3.

Table 5.3: Zumba Shakers data

Profile tab	
Item number	ZS
Item name	Zumba Shakers
I buy	5-1410
I sell	4-1410
Item details tab	
Description	Toning Sticks
Buying details tab	
Standard cost	7.50
Primary supplier for reorders	Health Food Supplies
Supplier item number	ZS100
Default reorder quantity	10
Selling details tab	
Base selling price	16.50

In MYOB you are able to build items from other items through criteria defined in the Item Information: Auto-Build window (see figure 5.11, overleaf). The Auto-Build feature enables the business to manage simple manufacturing processes and to monitor work in progress (WIP) and finished goods.

Figure 5.11: Item Information: Auto-Build window

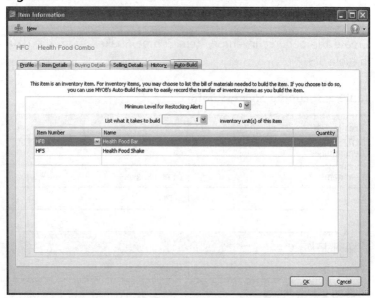

In our example, Health Food Combo consists of:

1   Health Food Bar

1   Health Food Shake

This could be auto-built when required from the inventory items in stock and sold at a special price. Note that only perpetual inventory that has the 'I inventory' option ticked can be selected for an auto-build item. The Item Information: Auto-Build window will show which inventory items are required to auto-build the new item. This is, in effect, a list of the ingredients required to create the item.

The field Minimum Level for Restocking Alert is sourced from the field of the same name in the Item Information: Buying Details window (see figure 5.8 on p. 171). The field 'List what it takes to build X inventory unit(s) of this item' is editable and reflects how many items will be created from the units listed. We will examine the Auto-Build feature in more detail later.

Exercise 5.4

Create five separate inventory items from the details in table 5.4.

Table 5.4: inventory data

Profile tab					
Item number	HFB	HFS	DP01AU	DY01AU	DM01AU
Item name	Health food bars	Health Food shakes	DVD Beginners pilates	DVD Beginners yoga	DVD Beginners martial arts
I buy	5-1420 Health food COS	5-1420 Health food COS	5-1430 DVD COS	5-1430 DVD COS	5-1430 DVD COS
I Sell	4-1420 Health food income	4-1420 Health food income	4-1430 DVD Income	4-1430 DVD Income	4-1430 DVD Income
I inventory	1-1420 Health food inventory	1-1420 Health food inventory	1-1430 DVD inventory	1-1430 DVD Inventory	1-1430 DVD Inventory
Item details tab					
Description	-	-	A 6 part beginners pilates DVD set	A 6 part beginners yoga DVD set	A 6 part beginners martial arts DVD set
Check use item description on sales and purchases					

Table 5.4: *(cont'd)*

Buying details tab					
Standard cost	$1	$1.66	$15	$15	$15
Tax code when bought	GST	GST	GST	GST	GST
Buying unit measure	Bars	Sachet	DVD	DVD	DVD
Minimum level for restocking	20	20	10	15	5
Primary supplier for reorders	Health food supplies		Fitness DVDs Australia		
Supplier item number	HB100	HFS100	DP01AU	DY01AU	DM02AU
Default reorder quantity	100	100	10	10	10
Selling details tab					
Base selling price	$2.50	$3.50	$39.95	$39.95	$39.95
Tax code when sold	GST	GST	GST	GST	GST
Selling unit of measure	HB	HFS	DVD	DVD	DVD

Exercise 5.5

Create a new inventory item that utilises the Auto-Build feature from the details in table 5.5. Select the Auto-Build tab and enter the data as per figure 5.11 (on p. 176).

Table 5.5: inventory data for

Profile tab	
Item number	HFC
Item name	Health food combo
I sell	4-1420 HEALTH FOOD Income
I inventory	1-1420 HEALTH FOOD Inventory
Item details tab	
Description	Lunch! Yummy health food bar and shake combo
Check use item description on sales and purchases	
Selling details tab	
Base selling price	$5.00
Tax code when sold	GST
Selling unit of measure	COMBO
Auto-build tab	
List what it takes to build X inventory unit(s) of this item	1
Item number + quantity	HFB + 1 HFS + 1

Item List

The Item List (see figure 5.12, overleaf) is found in the centre of the Inventory Command Centre flowchart (see figure 5.1 on p. 162) and is a list of all inventory items, detailing their number, name, QOH, last cost price and base selling price. Once an item has been used, it cannot be deleted and the link set-up cannot be amended, so this list can be quite long, depending on what you do with the inventory within your business.

Figure 5.12: Item List

Item Number	Name	On Hand	Last Cost		Sell Price	
DM01AU	DVD Beginners Martial Arts	200	$15.00	*	$39.95	*
DP01AU	DVD Beginners Pilates	200	$15.00	*	$39.95	*
DY01AU	DVD Beginners Yoga	200	$15.00	*	$39.95	*
HFB	Health Food Bar	55	$1.00	*	$2.50	*
HFC	Health Food Combo	10	$2.418	*	$5.00	*
HFS	Health Food Shake	55	$1.66	*	$3.50	*
Y	Yoga Mats	0	$0.00	*	$16.00	*
ZS	Zumba Shakers		$7.50	*	$16.50	*

From the Item List, you can create, edit and search for items. There is a variety of search options and a search field. The Advanced button has three additional fields, Description, Primary Supplier and Supplier Item Number, and four tabs, All Items, Sold, Bought and Inventoried, which reflect how the inventory was set up.

If an Item is not linked to 'I inventory', then there is no entry in the On Hand column, it is periodic inventory, and the stock quantity is not being recorded through MYOB.

Entering an inventory purchase

On day 4 we purchased inventory in the Purchase Command Centre. We are now going to revisit this area and process an inventory purchase in order to see the impact this has on purchasing periodic and perpetual inventory. In this example, Health Food Bars and Shakes (set up as perpetual inventory) and Zumba Shakers (set up as periodic inventory) will be purchased from the primary supplier Health Food Supplies.

Turbo Tip

Go to Menu Bar → Set-up → Preferences → Inventory tab and select the option Use Standard Cost as the Default Price on Purchase Orders and Bills, so that the cost pre-fills. This saves time and acts as a double-check when you are entering data.

Go to the Purchase Command Centre and click Enter Purchase, then enter Health Food Supplies in the Supplier field. The Item Layout is predefined in the Health Food Supplies set-up and is the only layout option that can be selected when purchasing inventory.

The date is 1 November 20XX and the supplier number is HFS1001.

The purchase consists of:

50 units of HFB-Health Food Bars

50 units of HFS-Health Food Shakes

10 units of ZS-Zumba Shakers

Before you record this transaction, go to the Menu Bar and click Edit → Recap Transactions to see the journal entry. This is shown in figure 5.13. Let's now take a close look at this journal entry, because once you understand it you will have a better understanding of perpetual and periodic inventory and the reporting consequences of each.

Figure 5.13: journal entry for purchase from Health Food Supplies

1/10/20XX Purchase; Health Food Supplies		
Auto# 2-1000 Trade Creditors		$208.00 (CR)
Auto# 1-1420 Health Food Inventory	$120.91 (DR)	
Auto# 5-1410 Equipment COS	$ 68.18 (DR)	
Auto# 2-4000 GST Paid		$ 19.36 (DR)

As with other purchases, the total amount has been credited to the liabilities account Trade Creditors. Once the bill is paid, Trade Creditors will be debited and the bank or credit card account will be credited.

The GST-exclusive value of the purchase of the HFB-Health Food Bars and HFS-Health Food Shakes has been debited to the asset account Health Food Inventory, increasing the value of the inventory account. This is because HFB and HFS are perpetual inventory items. If you looked at the balance sheet, you would see that the inventory has increased in value. If you looked at a profit and loss statement for the period when the transaction occurred, there would be no trace of this purchase.

The GST-exclusive value of the purchase of the ZS-Zumba Shakers has been directly debited to the Equipment Cost of Sales account, because Zumba Shakers are not linked to 'I inventory'. The Zumba Shakers stock is monitored on a periodic basis. If you looked at the balance sheet, you would not see any evidence of the Zumba Shakers purchase. If a stocktake was undertaken, the inventory value of the Zumba Shakers might be updated, but this transaction will not cause the inventory value to change. If you looked at a profit and loss statement for the period when the transaction occurred, you would see the purchase listed as a cost of sale. Note that it will appear as a cost of sale immediately. If it were perpetual inventory, it would appear as a cost of sale once a corresponding sale has in fact occurred.

The GST component has been recognised and posted to the GST Paid clearing account, and will be recovered when a BAS is prepared and submitted.

Now you can close the Recap Transaction window and click Record to record the purchase of the health food bars.

Exercise 5.6

In this exercise you will record a purchase order for DVDs and make a payment for the Health Food Supplies purchase.

1 Record purchase order number DF6973 from Fitness DVDs Australia, dated 1 November 20XX, for:

- 100 units of DP01AU

- 100 units of DY01AU

- 100 units of DM01AU

2 Process the payment for the Health Food Supplies purchase HFS1001 on 12 November 20XX from the ANZ bank account.

Recording receipt of goods delivered

As we discussed on day 4, items can be received without a supplier bill. For example, stock may be delivered to the warehouse accompanied by a delivery docket while the bill is sent directly to accounts payable. Because these documents are received at different times, the stock needs to be received without a corresponding supplier bill.

Let's suppose that a delivery of the following stock, accompanied by a delivery docket but no bill, has been received from Health Food Supplies on 15 November 20XX:

10 units of HFB-Health Food Bars

10 units of HFS-Health Food Shakes

10 units of ZS-Zumba Shakers

▶ Go to the Inventory Command Centre and click Receive Items, and a new purchase window will open. The background will be green, and at top left the Purchase Type will be displayed as RECEIVE ITEMS. Enter Health Food Supplies in the Supplier field. The date is 5/11/20XX. Leave the supplier invoice number blank, as it is not yet known.

▶ In the Purchases block, enter '10' in the Ordered column and then tab across and enter '10' in the Received column. Recording this transaction will create an order, and thus the quantity in the Ordered column needs to be equal to or greater than the quantity in the Received column. Select HFB in the Item Number column and tab through. The dollar value is not usually reported on the delivery docket. Tab through to the second row.

▶ Enter '10' in the Ordered column and tab across. Then enter '10' in the Received column and '10 HFS' in the Item Number column. Tab through to the third row.

▶ On the third row enter '10' in the Ordered column and tab across. Then enter '10' in the Received column and '10 ZS' in the Item Number column. You will notice that 'ZS' is not available on the drop-down list. The business is not recording the inventory of the Zumba Shakers, and so when a delivery arrives MYOB AccountRight is not set up to record the stock delivery of this item. Go back and remove the entries from the third line. On the Menu Bar click Edit → Insert Header, and in the Description column type '10 * Zumba Shakers', to recognise the delivery.

▶ Go to the Menu Bar and click Edit → Recap Transactions.

▶ An information window will pop up, requesting that you specify an account for item receipts. On day 4 you were introduced to the Purchased Command Centre linked accounts. In order to receive items without a supplier bill, the option 'I can receive items without a Supplier bill' must be checked and linked to the liability account '2-6500 Items Received'. Click OK, and the Purchase Linked Accounts window opens (shown in figure 4.2 on p. 127). Tick the box beside 'I can receive items without a Supplier bill' and tab to the Liability Account for Item Receipt field, and enter '2-6500'. Tab again and then click New, and create a new general ledger code, '2-6500 Items Received'. Click OK.

▶ Go to the Menu Bar and click Edit → Recap Transactions. Figure 5.14 shows the journal entry for the Health Food Supplies purchase.

Figure 5.14: journal entry for recording receipt of goods delivered

1/10/20XX Purchase; Health Food Supplies		
Auto# 2-6500 Items Received		$24.18 (CR)
Auto# 1-1420 Health Food Inventory	$24.18 (DR)	

The liability account Items Received has been credited (increased in value), as the business owes the supplier for the stock.

The asset account Health Food Inventory has been debited (increased in value) to recognise the additional stock.

There is no recognition of the Zumba Shakers, as they are periodic inventory and not linked to 'I inventory'.

▶ Click Record and then click Cancel. Recording this transaction has converted it to an order. Go to the Purchase Command Centre and click the Purchase Register and then the Orders tab.

The order you have just created can be seen in the Purchase Register window. There is no Supplier Inv No. and no dollar value, and on the far right-hand side the Received column has been ticked to indicate that the goods have been received. A Receive Items record no longer exists—it has been converted to a purchase order.

Exercise 5.7

Record a delivery of the following stock from Health Food Supplies on 15 November 20XX. No supplier invoice was provided.

> 15 units of HFB-Health Food Bars
>
> 15 units of HFS-Health Food Shakes

Entering an inventory sale

The sale of inventory is processed through the Sales Command Centre. We reviewed this area on day 4, but it will be useful to revisit it here to review a sale of inventory items and the implications of this.

Go to the Sales Command Centre, click Enter Sales and enter Fig Tree Gardens in the Customer field. If an existing quote or order pops up in a new window, click New Sale.

The sale dated 17 November 20XX, Customer PO No. FTOCT482, is for the following stock:

> 1 unit of HFB-Health Food Bars
>
> 1 unit of HFS-Health Food Shakes
>
> 1 unit of ZS-Zumba Shakers

Remember to select Item layout for the sale (see figure 5.15).

Figure 5.15: Sales New Item window

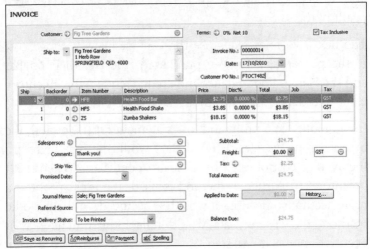

Go to the Menu Bar and click Edit → Recap Transactions. Figure 5.16 shows the journal entry for this transaction.

Figure 5.16: journal entry for an inventory sale to Fig Tree Gardens

17/10/20XX Sale; Fig Tree Gardens		
Auto# 1-5000 Trade Debtors	$24.75 (DR)	
Auto# 4-1420 Health Food Income		$ 6.00 (CR)
Auto# 4-1411 Equipment Income		$16.50 (CR)
Auto# 2-3000 GST Collected		$ 2.25 (CR)
Auto# 4-1420 Health Food Inventory		$ 2.45 (CR)
Auto# 4-1420 Health Food COS	$ 2.45 (DR)	

It looks rather complicated for a relatively simple sale. The Trade Debtors account has been debited (increased in value) to recognise that money is owed to the business.

The Health Food and Equipment Income lines recognise the GST-exclusive income value.

GST Collected recognises that $2.25 has been collected as a result of the sale.

The next two lines recognise the GST-exclusive average cost of the perpetual inventory purchased (the Health Food Bar and the Health Food Shake) and credit (reduce) the inventory value and debit (increase) the Health Food cost of sales.

If you looked at a profit and loss statement for the period, the income from the Health Food Bars would be matched with the average cost of sale of the Health Food Bars. When the 'I inventory' or perpetual method is used, the gross profit is a more accurate reflection of what has occurred. In the periodic method, the cost of sale would reflect the purchase as it occurred, not as it was sold.

Remember that the Zumba Shakers are not inventoried, and so their cost may not be reflected in the profit and loss statement for this period.

The perpetual inventory method is a fiddly and rather time-consuming method, and may not suit high-volume, low-value stock. The results may not be worth the time and effort involved. Each business has different requirements, and you may need to seek the advice of an MYOB Certified Consultant to determine the method best suited to your business.

Exercise 5.8

In exercise 5.6 on p. 183 you created a purchase order for Fitness DVDs Australia. Convert the purchase order to a bill and record the payment in full by a cheque dated 12 November 20XX.

Setting item prices

All businesses need to change their current selling prices from time to time, and there are a few short cuts in MYOB AccountRight software to help you do this.

Go to the Inventory Command Centre and click Set Item Prices, and the Set Item Prices window opens (see figure 5.17). All items that are sold (they are linked to 'I Sell This Item') are listed, and the Current Prices column can be edited.

Figure 5.17: Set Item Prices window

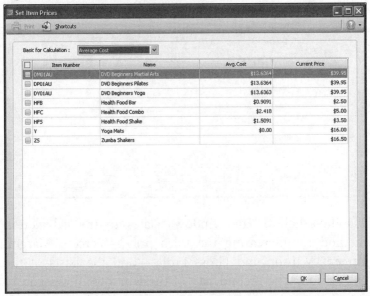

At the top of the window is the field Basis for Calculation, with two options: Average Cost and Last Cost. The Average Cost is the value of the item divided by the number of units on hand. The Last Cost is the last purchase price.

As noted, the selling price can be edited in the Current Price column, but when you want to edit a batch of selling prices you can use the short cuts. Check the items you want to update in the left-hand column and then click Shortcuts, and the Pricing Shortcuts window opens (see figure 5.18).

Figure 5.18: Pricing Shortcuts window

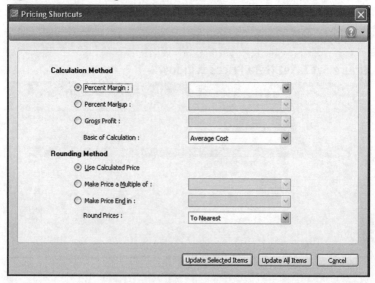

The first half of the window relates to the calculation method for increasing the sales price—Percent Margin, Percent Markup and Gross Profit—and the basis of the calculation. The second half of the window allows you to choose a rounding method. Make sure that you back up your data file before using this option in case the results are not as you wish.

Auto-Build items

You will recall that we discussed the Auto-Build feature earlier in this section with reference to the item HFC–Health Food Combo. To help you understand what is involved in auto-building, let's work through an example. Suppose that Fig Tree Gardens has ordered 10 Health Food Combos.

▶ Go to the Inventory Command Centre and click the Auto-Build Items button on the left-hand side (or use the shortcut Alt-A), and the Auto-Build Items window opens, with a list of any items that have auto-build capability. The columns are interchangeable, and the 'None' button at top left will reduce the Quantity to Build value to zero.

▶ In the Quantity to Build column on the Health Food Combo row, enter '10'. The unit entered must be a multiple of the figure entered in the field 'List what it takes to build X inventory unit(s) of this item'.

▶ Click the Build Items button.

▶ The Build Item window (see figure 5.19, overleaf) opens to display an inventory journal.

Figure 5.19: Build Item window

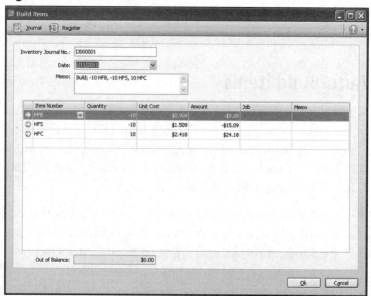

Enter 1 November 20XX in the Date field. The memo is automatically generated and can be edited. To explain this example, Build refers to the auto-build process. The notation '–10 HFB, –10 HFS' indicates that the stock levels for Health Food Bars and Health Food Shakes have each been reduced by 10 units.

Below the memo is the detail of the journal transaction movement. HFB and HFS have both been reduced by 10 units, and their dollar value has been reduced accordingly and transferred to inventory item HFC. A job and memo reference can be added here if appropriate.

Click Record, then click Cancel to close the Build Item window. If you go to the Item List, you will see that there are now 10 units of the HFC–Health Food Combo stock available to sell to Fig Tree Gardens.

Undertaking a stocktake

A stocktake is a count of the business inventory on hand. It is usually done at the end of the financial year, although some businesses may carry out stocktakes more regularly. As we noted earlier in this section, a periodic inventory system relies on stocktakes to update the Asset account, Inventory account and Cost of Sales account. Once the stocktake has been completed, the accountant can reconcile the physical stock and the inventory records and highlight any variances. Armed with accurate information about stock movements and stock on hand, the business owner can take the necessary action in regard to theft, slow-moving items, damaged stock, technological obsolescence and warehouse processes, and make informed decisions about the business's inventory.

▶ Clearly identify what stock is owned by the business and where it is. Separate stock that has been invoiced to a customer but is still in the warehouse. Likewise, stock received but not yet recorded in the books should be distinguished. Ensure that stock held at different locations or on consignment is accounted for.

▶ An inventory count sheet can be printed from MYOB AccountRight. Go to Reports → Inventory tab and select Inventory Count Sheet. Click Display; click Customise; click Report Fields and uncheck the On Hand field; and then click Display. This should produce a report of all inventory items, without the existing stock count as a reference. It is desirable that the stock counters are not influenced by the existing records.

▶ Ensure that the stockroom is clean and tidy and that inventory items are clearly laid out. It may be appropriate to attach labels to shelves to clearly identify different stock, such as 'inventory', 'inventory not to be counted' and so on. If appropriate, give the stock counters guidance as to how the count should be conducted; for example, 'Start at the top shelf and work your way down, and work from left to right'.

▶ Assemble the tools needed for the stocktake:

   ¤ Clipboards.

   ¤ Inventory count sheet. If inventory is barcoded, ensure that the stock sheets include barcodes.

   ¤ Write-off sheets. Check the condition of the inventory and write off any damaged or obsolete stock.

   ¤ Pens. The audit trail can be easily followed if the first counter uses a blue pen and the second counter uses a red pen, and the sheets are then submitted to the stocktake coordinator, who uses a purple pen.

   ¤ Calculators.

   ¤ Hand-held scanners for barcoded inventory.

▶ Discourage radios, mobile phones, iPods and idle chitchat, as distractions can easily lead to errors.

▶ Count every item of your inventory; don't estimate.

▶ Check the physical count against accounting records and recheck any discrepancies. Make a note of variances and follow up where necessary.

▶ Once the stocktake has been finalised, update the inventory records in your accounting package by adjusting the inventory.

Adjusting inventory

Inventory may need to be adjusted for a variety of reasons, including damage, theft and technological obsolescence, and it is useful to record these reasons in the adjustment journal. You can adjust both the unit and dollar value of inventory, but only do so for Items checked as 'I Inventory This Item'.

Before making an adjustment, it is prudent to check the current stock levels and values.

Click the Reports button on the Command Panel. Click the Inventory tab and select Items List Summary, and the Report Customisation window opens. Select the items under review and click Display. The report will provide details of the current stock level including the units on hand and the dollar value that has been recorded within MYOB AccountRight.

Exercise 5.9

The owners of Green Apple Gym have undertaken a stocktake and realise that they need to reduce the quantity of stock on hand as follows:

> 9 units of HFB-Health Food Bars—value $8.27
>
> 9 units of HFS-Health Food Shakes—value $13.73

▶ Go to the Inventory Command Centre and click Adjust Inventory, and the Adjust Inventory window opens (see figure 5.20, overleaf).

Figure 5.20: Adjust Inventory window

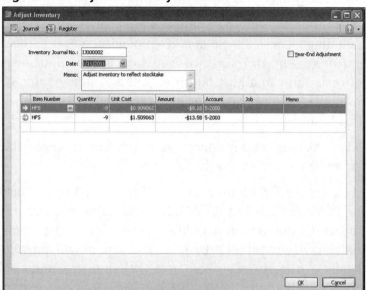

▶ Enter 01/11/20XX in the Date field.

▶ Enter 'Adjust inventory to reflect stocktake' in the Memo field.

▶ Leave the Year-End Adjustment window unchecked, as this adjustment is made during the financial year on 1 November 20XX.

▶ In the first row, enter HFB in the Item Number field, tab across, and enter '–9' in the Quantity column. It must be minus 9, as the value is being reduced. Tab across, and the Unit Cost and Amount columns should auto-fill.

▶ Tab through to the Account column. In this example the Cost of Sales account '5-2000 Stock Write-Offs' has been selected. The account selected will depend on the reason for the adjustment, and some businesses prefer to treat stock write-offs as an expense.

▸ In the second row, enter HFS in the Item Number field, tab across, and enter '–9' in the Quantity column. Tab across, and the Unit Cost and Amount columns should auto-fill. Go to the Menu Bar and click Edit → Recap Transactions, and the window will open to the journal entry shown in figure 5.21.

Figure 5.21: journal entry for adjusting inventory to reflect a stocktake

1/10/20XX Adjust inventory to reflect stocktake	
Auto# 5-2000 Stock Write-Offs $22.01 (DR)	
Auto# 1-1420 Health Food Inventory	$ 8.27 (CR)
Auto# 1-1420 Health Food Inventory	$13.73 (CR)

▸ This transaction has transferred the asset Health Food Inventory to the Cost of Sales account Stock Write-Offs. This will mean that the cost of the write-off is recognised in the profit and loss statement for the period.

▸ Click Record.

This transaction has processed an adjustment. You may wish to check the Items List Summary report to ensure that the correct adjustments have been made and that the desired values have been achieved.

A well-planned stocktake will result in minimal disruption and accurate inventory records, providing a sound basis for making informed business decisions.

Summary of day 5

Day 5 has introduced you to the Inventory Command Centre. To recap, we have covered the following topics: how to create inventory items, the concepts of perpetual and periodic inventory, how inventory is processed, how inventory is purchased and sold, assembling inventory through auto-builds, and undertaking stocktakes.

On day 6 we will explore the Payroll Command Centre, which offers a simple payroll management system. Note that the MYOB packages AccountRight Plus and upwards include the payroll function, whereas MYOB Business Basics and MYOB AccountRight do not include a payroll function.

Day 6

Payroll Command Centre

Key terms and concepts

▸ *PAYG withholding:* pay as you go withholding refers to the amount a business is obliged to withhold from the salary of its employees and remit to the ATO.

▸ *Annual leave:* a period of paid time off work that permanent employees are legally entitled to. In Australia most full-time employees are entitled to four weeks' **annual leave** after being employed for 12 months.

▸ *Personal leave:* paid time off work on account of illness or for personal reasons (such as bereavement or illness of a family member). **Personal leave** is an employee entitlement, but the amount varies according to the regulations that apply to different types of employment.

▸ *Superannuation guarantee charge (SGC):* the contribution employers are legally obliged to make to the superannuation fund of almost all their employees. The current rate is 9 per cent of the employee's ordinary earnings.

Introduction and overview

The Payroll Command Centre is a facility available in AccountRight Plus and later versions of MYOB AccountRight software. If you don't have this software and are not thinking of upgrading to it, you can skip this section and move on. If you are wondering whether it may be of interest to you, you may like to work through it in your trial version of the software to help you decide.

The Payroll Command Centre is designed to process a simple payroll. It has the ability to deal with activity slips and time sheets; to accrue entitlements; and to assist with the payment of PAYG withholding, superannuation and payroll tax. A particularly useful feature is that at the end of the payroll year it can produce payment summaries. To use this facility efficiently, you need to subscribe to payroll tax table updates and load them annually around 1 July.

To save money, some business owners who have a small workforce or a simple payroll decide that it's not worth the expense to upgrade to AccountRight Plus and struggle through the payroll process on their own. Others may have this software but be unwilling to subscribe to the tax table updates, electing instead to process the PAYG withholding payment manually. It's your decision, but if the hours and overtime your employees work often change, you will most likely find that the time you save by automating the process makes the upgrade a worthwhile investment. If your business has a complicated payroll involving up to 1000 employees, you may need to consider MYOB EXO Employer Services software. (Refer to the MYOB website for details.) When deciding on software for your business, you clearly have to weigh the expense against gains in efficiency and time saved.

Figure 6.1 shows the Payroll Command Centre flowchart.

Figure 6.1: Payroll Command Centre flowchart

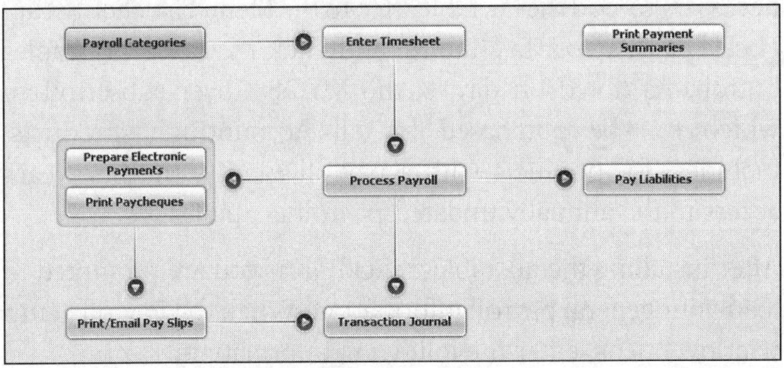

Our aim today is to give you an overview of the different elements of the Payroll Command Centre. You will learn how to operate the MYOB payroll system and which elements you can change when required. The area of payroll is subject to continuous legislative changes, which are beyond the scope of this book. Further information is available from government departments, such as Fair Work Australia or the ATO, or from your accountant or a payroll specialist.

The payroll process involves:

▶ setting up employee payroll details in the Employee Card and under Payroll Categories

▶ gathering all payroll information for the relevant pay period including authorised time sheets, leave of absence forms and so on

▶ processing payroll

▶ making payroll payments via Prepare Electronic Payments or Print Pay Cheques, or manually

▶ printing/emailing pay slips to employees.

Payroll set-up

The first time the Payroll Command Centre is viewed, it's necessary to load the tax tables. Go to the Menu Bar, click Setup, click Load Payroll Tax Tables, and click the Load Tax Tables button. As noted on day 1, the MYOB Cover subscription, which can be purchased for all AccountRight products, includes (for products with a payroll facility) the first year's access to the annually updated payroll tax tables.

After installing the tax tables, click OK if you are prompted to load your general payroll information. When the Payroll Setup window opens, enter the following information:

Current Payroll Year Ends: June 30, 20XX

Number of Hours in a Full-Time Work week: 38

Withholding Payer Number: (leave blank)

Round Net Pay Down to a Multiple of: 0

Default Superannuation Fund: Spectrum Super

Payroll categories

Go to the Payroll Command Centre and click the Payroll Categories button. Across the top of the Payroll Category List window you will see six tabs: Wages, Superannuation, Entitlements, Deductions, Expenses and Taxes (see figure 6.2).

Figure 6.2: Payroll Category List window

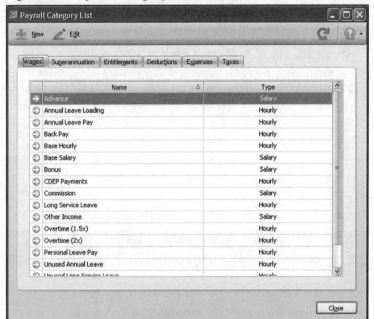

Wages

The frequently used categories in this area are Base Hourly, Annual Leave Pay (called Holiday Pay in older versions of AccountRight) and Personal Leave Pay (called Sick Pay in older versions of AccountRight). (The terms holiday pay and sick pay were replaced by annual leave pay and personal leave pay in the most recent legislation.) The MYOB data file has numerous Wage categories that you will probably never use. You can either edit them to suit your businesses payroll requirements or simply delete them.

Turbo tip

I recommend that you set up all employees as hourly employees, even if they are salaried. It is far easier to calculate variables such as annual leave when the calculation is based on hours rather than salary.

▶ Click Base Hourly, and the Wages Information: Base Hourly window opens (see figure 6.3). This is a straightforward window with fixed fields.

Figure 6.3: Wages Information: Base Hourly window

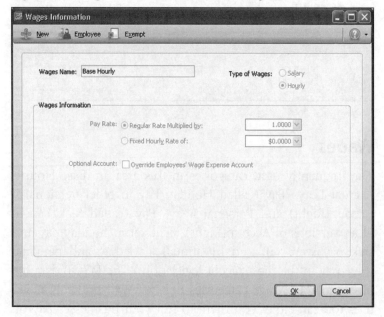

▶ Click OK and then click Annual Leave Pay to view the Wages Information: Annual Leave Pay window (see figure 6.4). The expense Annual Leave Pay will automatically flow through to the Employees Wage account. The Optional Account check box allows you to separate it and link it to its own specific general ledger account, but in my experience this is rarely done.

Figure 6.4: Wages Information: Annual Leave Pay window

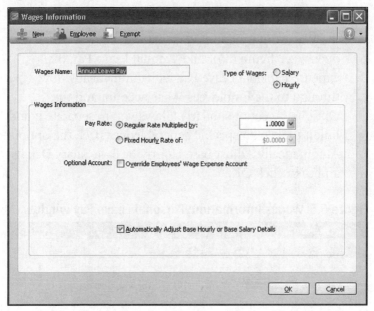

▶ Tick the option Automatically Adjust Base Hourly or Base Salary Details. This useful option was introduced in version 19 of AccountRight Plus. It allows MYOB to recognise when an employee is being paid for annual leave, and the system then adjusts the base pay accordingly. For example, if an employee usually works five days a week and in one week takes two days' holiday, when you process the pay you would enter the two days' holiday and the normal base pay will automatically be reduced to three days. Previously, you would have had to make this adjustment manually. If you are using an existing data file, check to see if these new boxes have been ticked. If they haven't, it's worth reviewing your business processes and asking yourself whether doing this would be of benefit to your business. I suspect it would.

▶ Now click OK and then click Personal Leave Pay, and the Wages Information: Personal Leave Pay window opens (see figure 6.5). Like Annual Leave Pay, the expense Personal Leave Pay will automatically flow through to the Employees Wage account and the Optional Account similarly allows you to separate it and link it to its own specific general ledger. Tick the option Automatically Adjust Base Hourly or Base Salary Details and then click OK.

Figure 6.5: Wages Information: Personal Leave Pay window

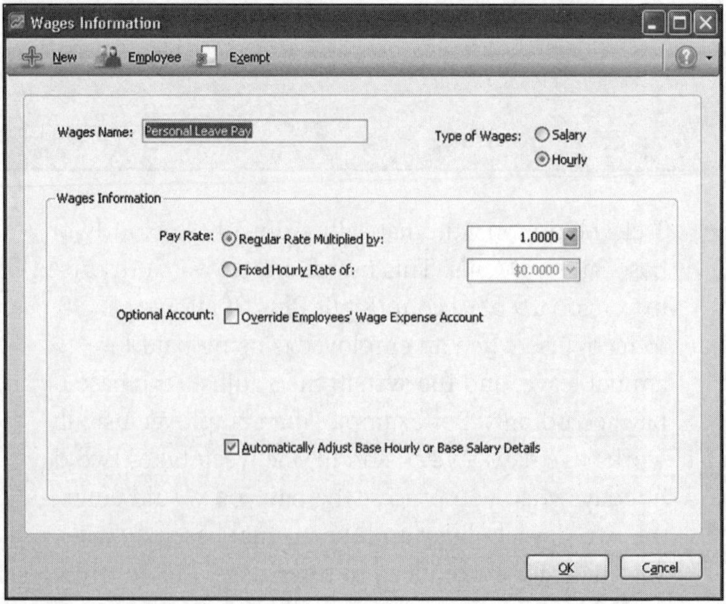

Exercise 6.1

Take some time to familiarise yourself with the various wage categories, noting those most relevant to your business.

Superannuation

The next aspect of payroll we need to consider is superannuation. In Australia, employers are legally obliged to contribute to the superannuation fund of almost all their employees. This is called the **superannuation guarantee charge (SGC)**. The government sets the rate, which is currently 9 per cent of the employee's gross salary or wages.

Click the Superannuation tab to open the Payroll Category List: Superannuation window (see figure 6.6).

Figure 6.6: Payroll Category List: Superannuation window

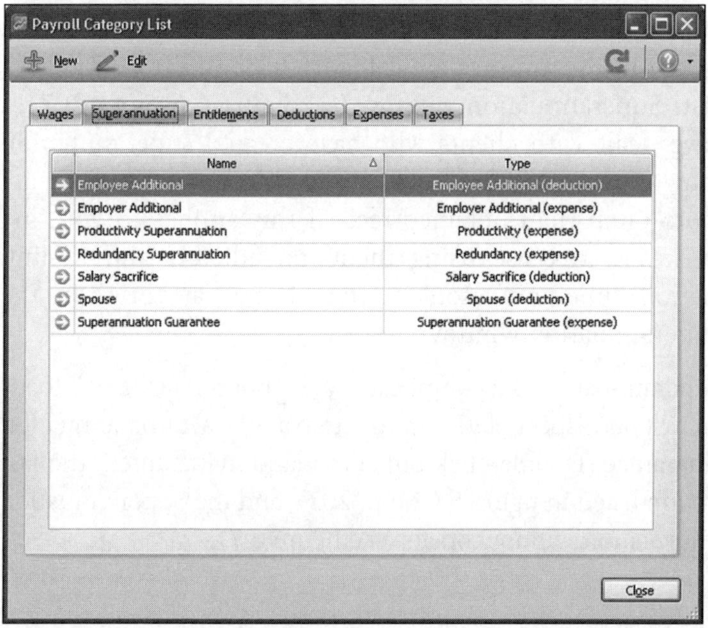

As the first step in processing this contribution, the business needs to select a default superannuation account. Go to Menu Bar → Setup → General Payroll Information → Default Superannuation Fund.

Next, a signed Superannuation Choice Form should be on file for all employees. All new employees should be issued with this form within 30 days of starting employment. This form can be printed off from MYOB AccountRight. Go to Menu Bar → Setup → General Payroll Information and select Create Superannuation Choice Form. It's a legal requirement that the employee be asked to sign a statement acknowledging that he or she has received the form and to keep a record of this signed statement. If an employee does not return the Superannuation Choice Form, his or her superannuation payments will be made to the business's selected default superannuation fund.

Both the employee and the employer can elect to make additional superannuation contributions, and it's most important that all superannuation-related payments be linked to the appropriate category in the Payroll Category List: Superannuation window (see figure 6.6 on p. 207). I have dealt with clients who have created superannuation categories in other areas, and unfortunately they are more often than not incorrect. If this applies to you, my advice is to cease using them immediately and to link payroll superannuation to one of the categories in the Superannuation window.

Superannuation is a complicated area, but today we will focus on just one aspect of it: how to set up a typical Superannuation Guarantee. Double-click Superannuation Guarantee (the last option listed in figure 6.6 on p. 207), and the Superannuation Information window opens (see figure 6.7).

Figure 6.7: Superannuation Information window

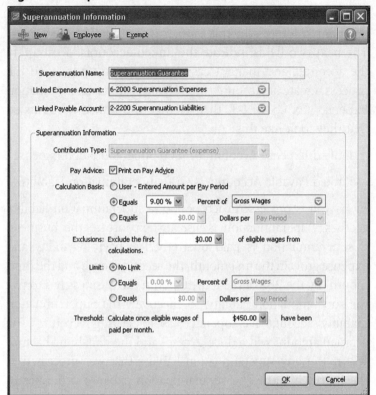

Along the top you will see the Employee button, which lists all employees. A tick in the check box indicates that they qualify for this superannuation. Superannuation is only paid on ordinary time earnings (OTE), so all other wage categories need to be exempted from the calculation via the Exempt button. There are two areas where people often go wrong, so watch out for them:

▶ A bonus based on work performed attracts superannuation; other bonuses don't.

▶ Accrued lump sum payments for long service leave or annual leave don't attract superannuation.

The first field in the Superannuation Information window is Name. This identifies the category to which the superannuation payment belongs—in this case, Superannuation Guarantee. The next two fields indicate the linked accounts. To simplify the accounts and make it easier for users to understand the process, create an account, 6-5200 and call it Superannuation Expense, tax code N-T, then change the linked accounts so that they look like this:

Linked Expense Account: 6-5200 Superannuation Expense

Linked Payable Account: 2-2200 Superannuation Liabilities

As payroll is processed each period, a superannuation liability accrues. Superannuation is also an expense to the business. If superannuation is paid quarterly, the payroll liability and expense grow in the first month, the second month and the third month. By the 28th of the fourth month the business has to pay the superannuation liability, so effectively the Superannuation Liability account has operated as a clearing account. The accrued amount will reduce to zero, and the remaining balance will reflect any superannuation liability that was processed in the fourth month. The superannuation expense continues to grow, while the superannuation liability clears every quarter.

Below the linked accounts is an area called Superannuation Information. It's a legal requirement that superannuation be printed on the Pay Advice slip, so you will see that this box is already ticked.

The Calculation Basis is set at 9 per cent of gross wages. This field is editable, to allow for legislative changes.

The Exclusions and Limit fields allow you to exclude a portion of the wages from the calculations or to set a limit on the superannuation payment respectively. For example, superannuation is not calculated on overtime or bonuses.

The Threshold field is set at $450, since currently superannuation is not paid until gross wages have reached $450 within the month, but this field is editable.

It's not necessary to set up a separate superannuation category for each individual superannuation fund, as all employees are linked to a single SGC Superannuation category and their actual fund is defined in their Employee Card. The individual superannuation funds are set up elsewhere. Go to the Menu Bar and click Lists → Superannuation Fund. Click New at top left, and a blank Edit Superannuation Fund window opens. Complete the fields as shown in figure 6.8 and then select OK.

Figure 6.8: Edit Superannuation Fund window

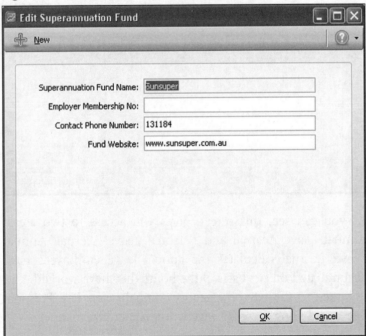

Entitlements

Now let's take a look at how we process employee entitlements within the payroll area. Employee entitlements are things like annual and personal leave, and are listed by category in the Payroll Category List: Entitlements window (see figure 6.9).

Figure 6.9: Payroll Category List: Entitlements window

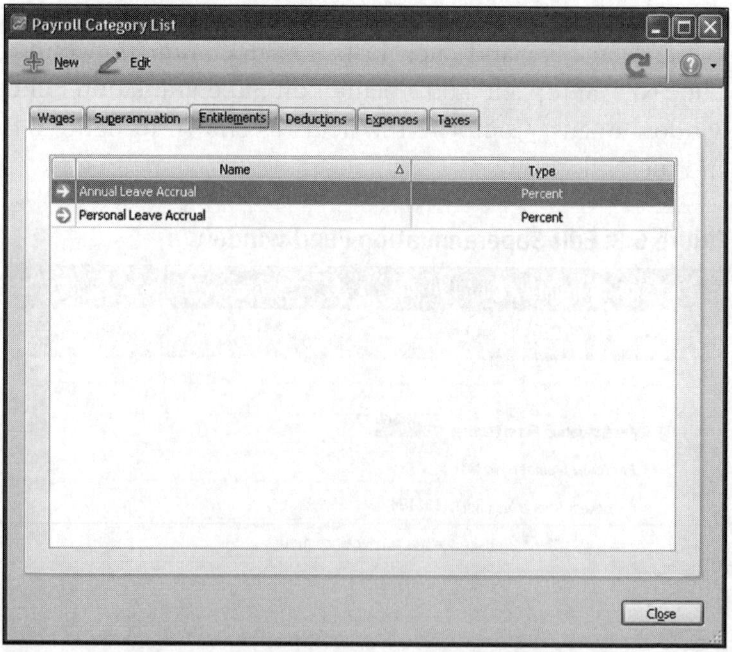

As you can see, this screen gives you access to two areas: Annual Leave Accrual and Personal Leave Accrual. Annual Leave Accrual calculates the annual leave employees have accumulated on the basis of the hours they have worked, and is linked to the payroll category Annual Leave Pay. Personal Leave and Long Service Leave work in a similar manner.

To explore this area, double-click Annual Leave Accrual, and the Payroll Category List: Entitlements Information window opens (see figure 6.10). At the top of the screen are three buttons: New, Employee and Exempt. The New button allows you to create a new entitlement category, such as Long Service Leave, that is not created with the data file. The Employee button accesses all employees linked to this entitlement. The Exempt button brings up a list of all the wage categories, and you need to tick those that are excluded from the calculation.

Figure 6.10: Entitlements Information: Annual Leave Accrual window

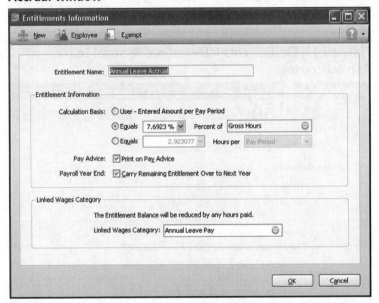

As noted earlier, I recommend that you set up all employees as hourly workers. Most businesses elect to record accrued leave as a percentage of hours worked (rather than hours per pay period). For example, a typical employee working a 38-hour week is entitled to 20 days' annual leave and accrues leave at a rate of

7.6923 per cent of total hours worked, as shown in figure 6.10. Table 6.1 sets out how this percentage is calculated.

Table 6.1: calculation of rate at which annual leave accrues for a typical full-time employee

Total hours of annual leave	=	20 days × 7.6 hours	=	152	
Total hours worked per year	=	52 weeks × 38 hours	=	1976	= 7.6923%

Similarly, in accordance with recent legislative changes our typical employee working a 38-hour week would be entitled to 10 days' personal leave (up from eight days), and would accrue personal leave at a rate of 3.84615 per cent of total hours worked, as shown in figure 6.11.

Figure 6.11: Entitlements Information: Personal Leave Accrual window

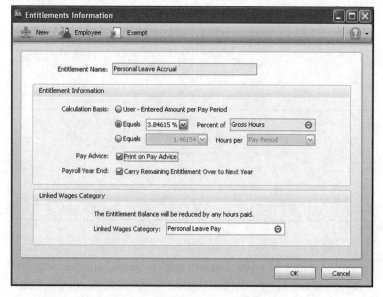

Table 6.2 sets out how this percentage is calculated.

Table 6.2: calculation of rate at which personal leave accrues for a typical full-time employee

Total hours of annual leave per year	=	10 days × 7.6 hours	=	76	= 3.84615%
Total hours worked per year	=	52 weeks × 38 hours	=	1976	

The figures shown in these calculations are for illustrative purposes only. Clearly, the percentage will vary according to the criteria. The important point for our purposes is that once you have entered the relevant data for the employees of your business, MYOB will automatically calculate the leave each has accrued and adjust the pay accordingly.

In figures 6.10 (on p. 213) and 6.11 you will have noticed two check box options: one to print the information on the Pay Advice and the second to carry the remaining entitlement over to the next year. Under Australia's Modern Awards, both Annual Leave Accrual and Personal Leave Accrual must be printed on the Pay Advice, and it will depend on the agreements in place as to whether a particular employee's entitlement can be carried over into the next payroll year.

Exercise 6.2

Certain wage categories need to be exempted from the personal leave accrual calculations. Go to the Payroll Command Centre, click Payroll Categories, click the Entitlements tab, click Personal Leave Accrual and click the Exempt button, and then select the following:

  Overtime (1.5x)

  Unused Holiday Pay

  Unused Long Service Leave

  Annual Leave Loading

Finally, click OK to return to the Payroll Category List: Entitlements window.

Deductions

The Payroll Category List: Deductions window (see figure 6.12) allows you to set up deductions from an employee's wages, such as the cost of an employee purchase (for example, a laptop for private use) or a one-time deduction (for example, a loan to the employee from the business, or a union fee). The various deductions are entered as a percentage or a whole-dollar amount as shown, and can be linked to a relevant account.

Figure 6.12: Payroll Category List: Deductions window

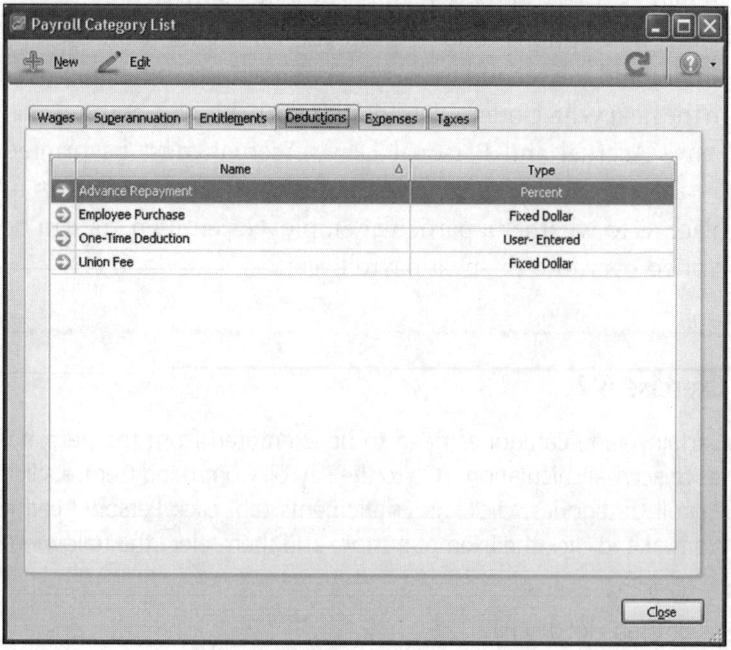

Expenses

In all my years of working with MYOB, I have never used the Expenses tab of the Payroll Category List (see figure 6.13). If, however, the business incurs an expense on an employee's behalf, this area can be used to record it.

Figure 6.13: Payroll Category List: Expenses tab

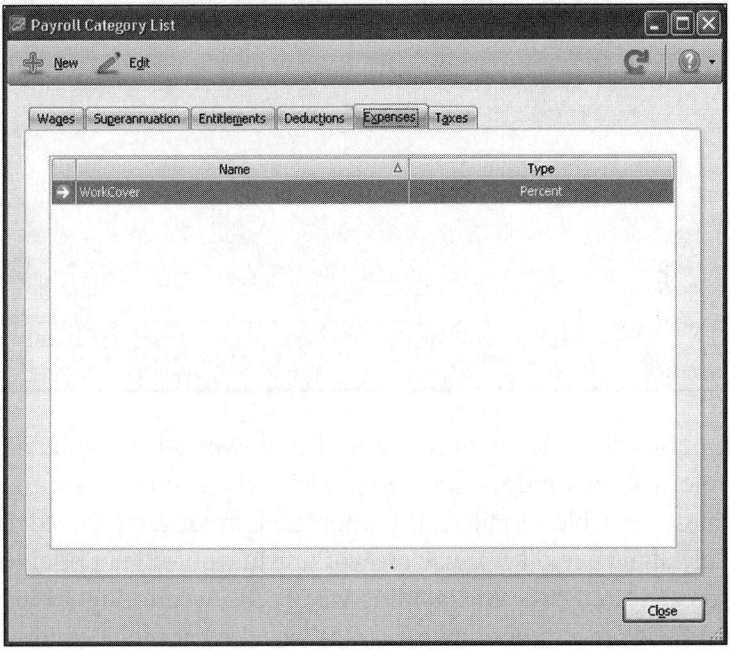

Taxes

The Taxes tab of the Payroll Category List window gives you access to the PAYG Withholding linked account (see figure 6.14, overleaf).

Figure 6.14: Payroll Category List: Taxes window

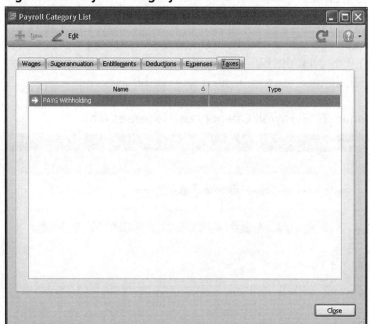

Double-click the zoom arrow to drill down to the Tax Table Information window (see figure 6.15). Here you will see the latest tax table installed. If it's not the current table, dated 1 July of the payroll year you are working in, you will not be able to calculate PAYG Withholding via MYOB AccountRight Plus and will have to do it manually (as we noted at the beginning of today's session).

If you click the field below the Tax Table Revision Date, you can see the various tax tables available. However, tax tables are selected in the employee's individual card file, not here.

Figure 6.15: Tax Table Information window

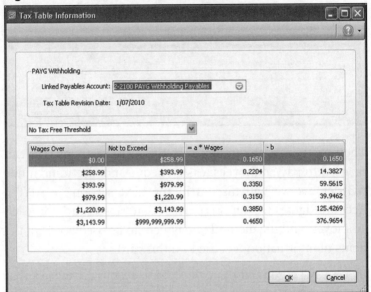

Payroll Linked Accounts

Payroll has six linked accounts. To view them, go to the Menu Bar and click Setup → Linked Accounts → Payroll Accounts, and the Payroll Linked Accounts window will open (see figure 6.16, overleaf).

Figure 6.16: Payroll Linked Accounts window

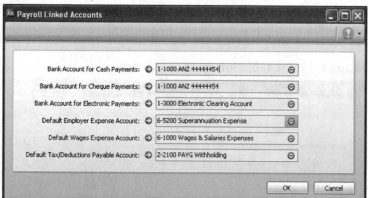

The first three accounts relate to the three methods that can be used to pay employees: cash, cheque and electronic funds transfer. As we will discuss in the next section, in MYOB AccountRight Plus an Employee Card is set up for each employee, and the method of payment to be used is one of the items of information recorded on this card.

If you pay payroll out of just one bank account, I suggest that you link the first two accounts to this bank account. This avoids errors, such as an employee accidentally being linked to the Cash payment option instead of the Cheque payment option.

The third option sometimes confuses users because when they use online banking to pay employees they refer to it as electronic banking. In MYOB AccountRight, electronic banking occurs when electronic payments are created within the

MYOB software and uploaded to the bank. The bank account for electronic payments is linked to the Electronic Clearing Account. The Default Employer Expense Account should be linked to the Superannuation Expenses account, 6-5200. Make the change now. The Default Wages Expense Account is linked to the standard Wages and Salaries Expenses account. The final field, Default Tax/Deductions Payable Account, is linked to the liabilities account PAYG Withholding Payables.

You will see what effect these linked accounts have as payroll is processed.

Setting up Employee Cards

We introduced the concept of the Employee Card File on day 1. Payroll Categories should be set up to deal with the general requirements relating to employment (see the Payroll Command Centre flowchart, figure 6.1 on p. 201), while the specific details of each person's employment conditions should be entered in the Employee Card File.

To set up an Employee Card, go to the Card File Command Centre and click Card List, then click the fourth tab along, the Employee tab. Double-click 'Bostick, Rosemary' to open up her card file (see figure 6.17, overleaf). We created Rosemary Bostick's employee card on Day 2. Across the top you will see six tabs: Profile, Card Details, Payroll Details, Payment Details, Contact Log and History.

Figure 6.17: Employee Card: Profile window

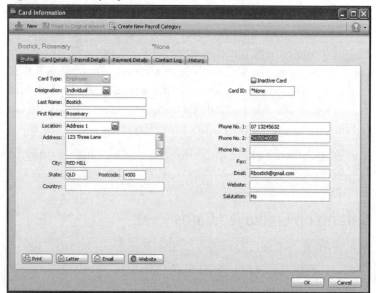

The Profile tab contains the employee's address and contact information. I usually enter the employee's tax file number in the Card ID field as a double-check that the business has the tax file number. This number is stored elsewhere, in the Payroll Details Tax tab, but if you enter it here you can quickly look at the file if it exists, and if not, you will know that this important data is missing. If you have young employees, it may be useful to include their parents' address in the Address 2 field. Most fields are self-explanatory.

At the bottom you will see four buttons: Print, Letter, Email and Website. Provided you have MAPI-compliant email software installed on your computer, the Email button enables you to email the employee directly.

The Card Details tab (see figure 6.18) allows you to store additional details about the employee such as a photo, notes and customised information. It's a simple matter to take a photo with an inexpensive webcam and upload it to the Employee Card File.

There are seven fields for adding customised information, an area we discussed on day 1. You can tailor this information to suit your business requirements. To access these fields for editing purposes, go to the Menu Bar and click Lists → Custom Lists and Field Names → Employees.

Figure 6.18: Employee Card: Card Details window

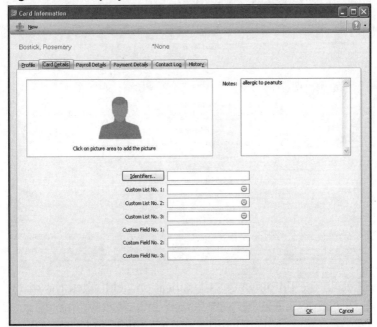

Next click the Payroll Details tab (see figure 6.19, overleaf). Along the left-hand side you will see a wizard with 10 tabs: Personal Details, Wages, Superannuation, Entitlements, Deductions, Employer Expenses, Taxes, Standard Pay, Pay History and Time Billing.

The Personal Details window is pretty much self-explanatory (see figure 6.19). The Calculated Age fills out automatically based on the Date of Birth. It's a legal requirement that the Employment Classification or job title be included on the employee's pay slip.

Figure 6.19: Payroll Details: Personal Details window

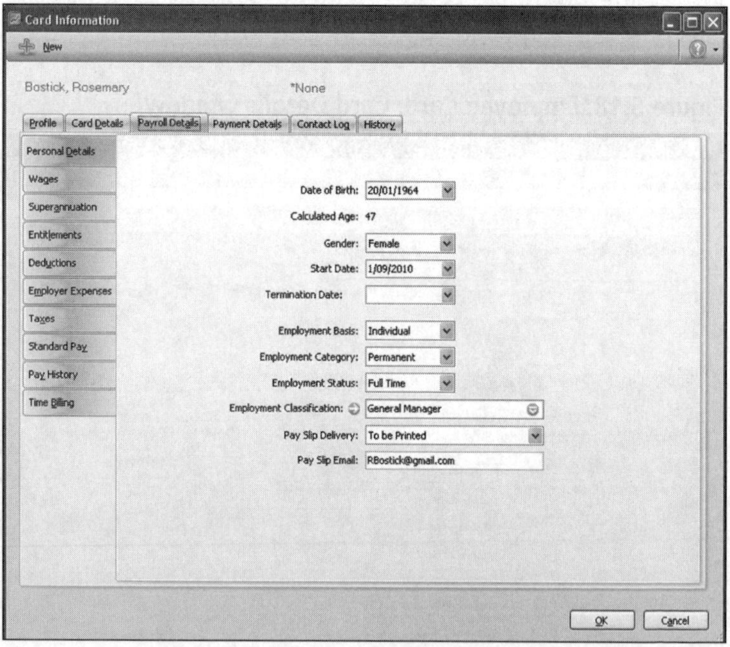

Click in the Employment Classification field, click the drop-down arrow, click the New button, enter a new Employment Classification (which will be the job title), and click OK. A quirk of this area is that you now have to go back and select the job title that was just created. (Of course, if the job title has already been created, it's not necessary to create another one.)

The Pay Advice can be printed or emailed to the employee. Emailing is quick and efficient, but you need to be aware that the address to which it is to be emailed might be different from the email address on the Employee Card: Profile tab (see figure 6.17 on p. 222). For privacy reasons you need your employees' written permission to email them their payroll advice.

The Wages tab (see figure 6.20) is where you enter details of the employee's wages. As I have noted several times, I recommend that you always use an hourly Pay Basis. Notice that the Annual Salary field is inactive. If you know the employee's salary but not the hours, select the appropriate Pay Frequency, enter the hours in the Pay Period field, change the Pay Basis to Salary, Enter the salary in the Annual Salary field, and then change the Pay Basis back to Salary—and the Hourly Rate will automatically be calculated.

Figure 6.20: Payroll Details: Wages window

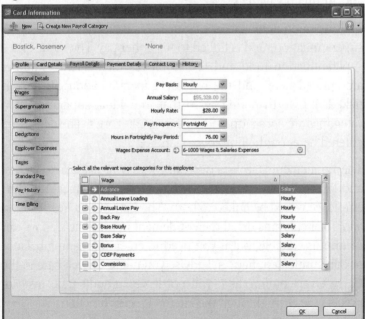

Currently the standard working hours are 38 per week. This figure is multiplied, depending on the Pay Period selected.

Below the wage fields in this window you will see the field Wages Expense Account, where you enter the account to which the individual wage expense is linked. If the wage expense is administrative in nature (for example, a receptionist's wage), it should be linked to an Expense account (6-XXXX). If it's related to providing a service (for example, a personal trainer's wage), it should be linked to a Cost of Sale account (5-XXXX), as it should be reflected in gross profits.

The wage categories in figure 6.20 (on p. 225) are sourced from the Payroll Category List: Wages (see figure 6.2 on p. 203). You may wish to simplify this list by deleting the wage categories your business will never use. Typically, a full-time employee is linked to Base Hourly, Annual Leave Pay and Annual Leave Pay.

The Superannuation tab (see figure 6.21) is where the employee's superannuation fund is linked to his or her pay. The name of the superannuation fund and the employee membership number are entered here, and the relevant superannuation category is ticked. It's worth noting again that individual superannuation categories are *not* set up under Payroll Categories. The details are entered here, on the Employee Card.

The Entitlements tab lists two categories, Annual Leave Accrual and Personal Leave Accrual (see figure 6.22). A typical full-time employee would be linked to both. The Carry Over, Year-to-Date and Total columns detail the entitlement hours. The Carry Over column is editable, but if you need to enter an opening balance or edit entitlement figures, I advise you not to do that here in the Carry Over column, as it will not leave an audit trail. Instead, process the entry through the Payroll Process function.

Figure 6.21: Payroll Details: Superannuation window

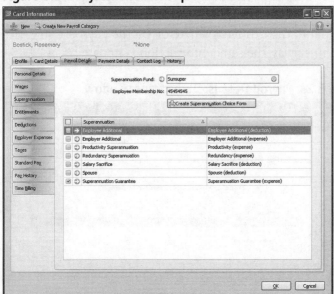

Figure 6.22: Payroll Details: Entitlements window

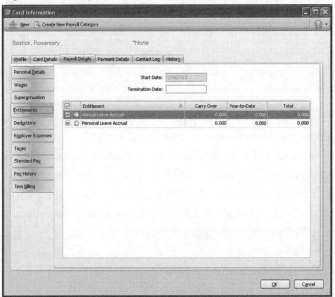

The Deductions tab (see figure 6.23) brings up a list of the four types of deductions mentioned earlier. The employee can be linked to the deductions here or via the Payroll Categories area. Either way, the same information is updated.

Figure 6.23: Payroll Details: Deductions window

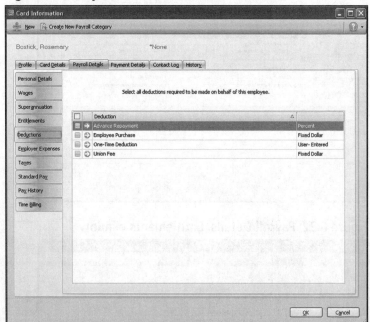

The Employer Expenses tab (see figure 6.24) accesses an area I have not seen anyone utilise in Australia (as I noted earlier), although I have heard of MYOB users overseas using these categories. The reference to WorkCover is misleading, as different states process WorkCover differently, and while this function was formerly useful in some states, my sources inform me that it is no longer applicable.

Figure 6.24: Payroll Details: Employer Expenses window

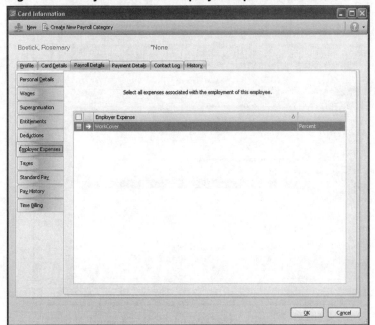

The Taxes tab (see figure 6.25, overleaf) is where you enter the information from the Tax file number declaration form (NAT 3092) that the employee submitted on starting employment. The relevant tax table is selected and variations or alterations to the PAYG Withholding can be entered here.

The Standard Pay tab provides a view of the employee's typical pay slip (see figure 6.26, overleaf). There is a customisable Memo field, where you can add the employee's name so that it will appear as a reference in the journal entry in the Transaction Journal. If the employee's standard pay was for 16 hours a week, you would overtype the 38 hours with 16 and this would automatically flow through to the processed payroll. Similarly, if the employee wished to make a regular additional superannuation contribution, or perhaps pay instalments on a laptop purchase, this would be entered here.

Figure 6.25: Payroll Details: Taxes window

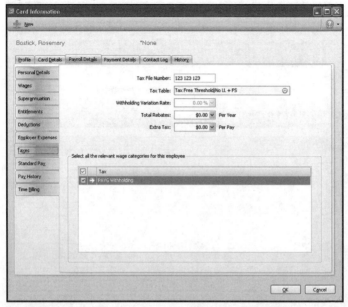

Figure 6.26: Payroll Details: Standard Pay window

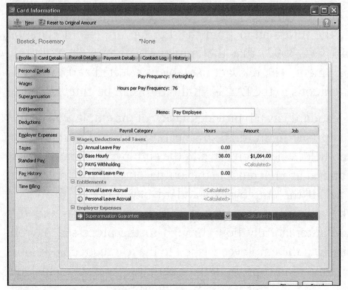

The Pay History tab is pretty much self-explanatory (see figure 6.27). The 'Show Pay History for' field offers a number of options, including monthly and quarterly. You can access similar information by clicking the Analysis button on the Command Panel when the Payroll Command Centre is active.

Figure 6.27: Payroll Details: Pay History window

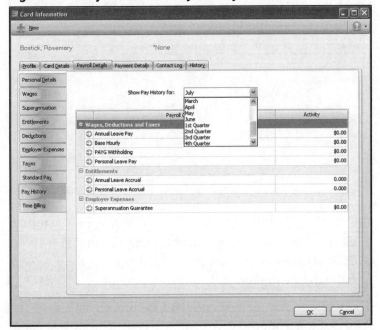

The Time Billing tab is used by consulting-type businesses, where fees are based on time (see figure 6.28, overleaf). The Employee Billing Rate is entered here. This information flows through to chargeable hourly Activities, and can be selected when Time Billing is used.

Figure 6.28: Payroll Details: Time Billing window

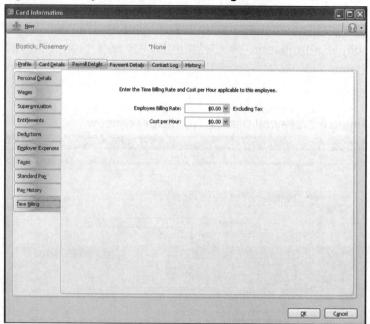

You will recall that the Payroll Linked Accounts window gives you three separate payment options (see figure 6.16 on p. 220). These options can be selected here on the Payment Details tab (see figure 6.29).

The first and second options have both been linked to the same bank account and refer to a payment from that bank account. The third option, Electronic, refers to an electronic payment processed *within* MYOB AccountRight. This creates an '.aba' bank file, which is uploaded to the business bank, as we discussed in detail on day 2. Many people mistakenly select the Electronic option when the Cheque or Cash option should be selected.

Figure 6.29: Payment Details window

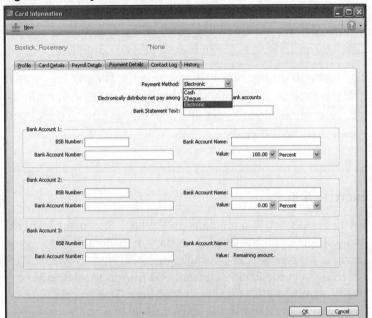

The Electronic payment option is an efficient method of processing payments and should seriously be considered. Using this option, the salary can be divided into three, by percentage or dollar value, and paid into three separate bank accounts. For example, some employees may wish to split their pay between their current, saving and home loan accounts. This may cost the business banking fees, but it provides a benefit to the employees. If the Cheque option is used, the bank details can still be stored in the Electronic option fields for future reference.

The business's details are entered in the Bank Statement Text field and will appear on the employee's bank statement, indicating the source of the payment.

Like other types of cards, the Employee Card has a Contact Log tab. Useful information like birthdays and start dates can be entered here via a new log entry and will activate a contact alert on the To Do List, which we will cover on day 7.

The final tab on the Employee Card is the History tab, which gives you access to the total monthly payments to the employee for the current payroll year and also allows you to select and view other payroll years.

Exercise 6.3

The business's details are entered in the Bank Statement Text field and will appear on the employee's bank statement, indicating the source of the payment. For example, you could enter WAGES GREEN APPLE GYM in the Bank Statement Text field so the employee can clearly identify the payment as wages from Green Apple Gym on their own bank statement. The field is limited to 18 characters and only appears as capital letters. Like other types of cards, the Employee Card has a Contact Log tab. Useful information like birthdays and start dates can be entered here via a new log entry and will activate a contact alert on the To Do List, which we will cover on day 7.

The final tab on the Employee Card is the History tab, which gives you access to the total monthly payments to the employee for the current payroll year and also allows you to select and view other payroll years. Enter the employee information for Rosemary Bostick found in figures 6.17 through to 6.29. Make sure that you include Rosemary's Profile information, her Card Details, Payroll Details and Payment Details. In the Contact Log enter a birthday reminder for next year. For further practice you could set up an additional employee, create their profile based on yourself, or an imaginary employee.

Exercise 6.4

Create three new Employee Cards using the details in table 6.3.

Table 6.3: new employee details for exercise 6.4

Profile tab			
Last name	Jones	Brown	Stella
First name	Tania	Marcia	Simpson
Payroll: personal details			
Date of birth	12/5/69	13/8/1971	13/4/1984
Gender	Female	Female	Male
Start date	1/10/20XX	1/10/20XX	1/10/20XX
Employment basis	Individual	Individual	Individual
Employment category	Permanent	Permanent	Temporary
Employment status	Full time	Part time	Casual
Employment classification	Personal trainer	Personal trainer	Assistant
Pay slip delivery	To be emailed	To be emailed	To be emailed
Pay slip email	tj@gmail.com	mb@gmail.com	ss@gmail.com
Payroll details: wages			
Pay basis	Hourly	Hourly	Hourly
Hourly rate	40.00	21.00	13.45
Pay frequency	Fortnightly	Fortnightly	Fortnightly
Hours in pay period	76.00	76.00	38.0
Wage expense account	5-3000	5-3000	6-1000
	Base hourly Annual leave pay Personal leave pay	Base hourly Annual leave pay Personal leave pay	Base hourly

Table 6.3: *(cont'd)*

Payroll: superannuation			
Last name	Jones	Brown	Stella
First name	Tania	Marcia	Simpson
Superannuation fund	SunSuper	Spectrum Super	SunSuper
Employee membership no:	123456	456123	789456
Select superannuation guarantee			
Payroll details: entitlements			
	Annual leave accrual Personal leave accrual	Annual leave accrual Personal leave accrual	
Payroll details: taxes			
Tax file number (remember to add the TFN to the Card ID)	124578457	895623855	785625625
Tax table	Tax free threshold/ no LL	Tax free threshold/ no LL + HECS or HELP	No tax free threshold
Select PAYG withholding			
Payroll: standard pay			
Base hourly		Delete 76.0 and enter 45.6	Delete 38.0
Payment details			
Payment method	Cheque	Cheque	Cheque

Processing the payroll

Payroll is usually a significant expense for a business, so it's very important to process it correctly. Before you start the payroll process, you should gather all payroll information for the relevant pay period.

Exercise 6.5

▶ Go to the Payroll Command Centre and click Process Payroll, and the Process Payroll: Pay Period tab opens (see figure 6.30). The four-step wizard along the left-hand side—Pay Period, Employee Pays, Process Payments and Pay Slips—will help you to work through the payroll process. You can work backward and forward through the payroll wizard so don't feel trapped when you start it. If you choose to close the payroll wizard before you have fully processed a payroll you will be given the option to save the pay run to process later.

Figure 6.30: Process Payroll: Pay Period tab

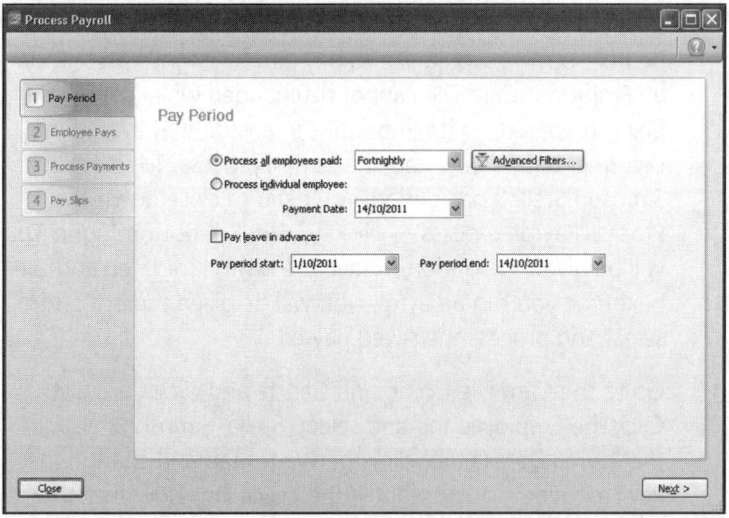

▶ Enter details about the actual pay period. In the field 'Process all employees paid', select Fortnightly. Enter the following dates:

Payment Date:	14 October 20XX
Pay period start:	1 October 20XX
Pay period end:	14 October 20XX

This means that the payroll payment will be made on 14 October. Note that this must be the date on which the business actually makes the payment. The payment is for a period of a fortnight, from 1 October to 14 October. There is a check box option that allows you to pay leave in advance, and it will correctly calculate tax for the period.

▶ Click the Next button at bottom right. Notice that as you do this that the Employees tab becomes active, changing to green. There should be four employees listed, but as 'Stella, Simpson' was linked to a weekly wage; he is not listed with this fortnightly pay. If he is in fact paid weekly, this would be fine, but we would like to pay him fortnightly. Details on an Employee Card File cannot be changed while payroll is being prepared, so it's important to ensure that everything is correct before you start the payroll process. To change Simpson Stella's pay period, you need to close down the Process Payroll process by clicking Close at bottom right. You will be given the option to save the payroll for later, and the next time you run a payroll, you will be given the option to select and process the saved payroll.

▶ Go to the Card File Command Centre and click Card List. Click the Employee tab and select 'Stella, Simpson'; click the Payroll Details tab; click the Wages tab and change the Pay Frequency to Fortnightly; then click OK. Now that this correction has been made, you need to go to the Standard Pay tab and delete the figure 76 in the Hours column. Remember that Simpson is a casual worker and does not work predefined hours.

▶ Now go back to step 1 and work through the Process Payroll process until you are up to the Process Payroll: Employee Pays tab and four employees are listed (see figure 6.31). A window will open, and you will be asked if you want to process the saved payroll: click continue to do so. I recommend that you un-tick all employees and check their pay one by one, and then re-tick them once you are satisfied that they are correct. Click the white zoom arrow to review and edit the employees' pay. Notice that Simpson Stella's pay has come through as zero. He is a casual employee and his standard pay details are set as zero. If you are using a different version of the annually updated tax tables, your figures may be slightly different to the figures shown.

Figure 6.31: Process Payroll: Employee Pays tab

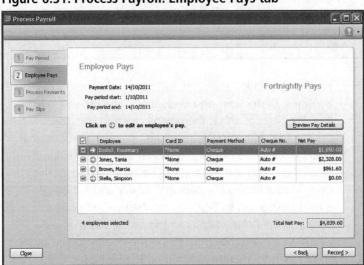

▶ Click 'Brown, Marcia' to see the details of her pay (see figure 6.32, overleaf). In the Memo field type in 'Marcia Brown Pay'. In the block below are Marcia Brown's payroll details.

Figure 6.32: Pay Employee window: payroll details for Marcia Brown

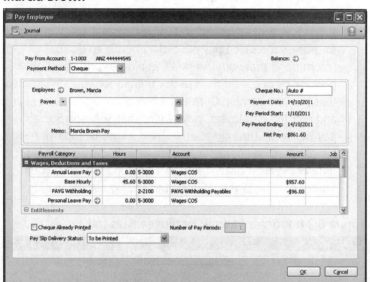

▸ The first group in the Payroll Category column in figure 6.32 is Wages, Deductions and Taxes. Looking at the Base Hourly row, the first column is the payroll category, the second column (disregarding the zoom arrow column) shows the hours worked (45.60), and the third and fourth columns detail the account the wage will be expensed to. In this case, Marcia Brown is a personal trainer and her wage is being expensed to 5-3000, the Wages Cost of Sales account. The Amount column shows the pay that is due, which is calculated by multiplying the hours worked by the employee's hourly rate as listed on the Employee Card. You can click the zoom arrow beside the employee's name to view details, but the details cannot be changed once you have started to process the payroll.

PAYG Withholding is the amount the business is obliged to deduct from the employee's wage and pay to the ATO on the employee's behalf. The calculation is linked to the tax rate specified in the Employee Card. This means that employees may receive the same gross wage, but because of a different tax rate—due to various factors, such as the Higher Education Contribution Scheme (HECS), residency status, and age—will be taxed a different amount, and so the net pay will be different. The PAYG Withholding Payables account is linked to the liability account PAYG Withholding. The amount is negative because it is deducted from the employee's gross wage.

The next section, which is out of view in this screen shot, is for Entitlements. The numbers represent the hours accrued from working the base hours—in this case, 45.60 hours.

The third section is for superannuation. As we discussed earlier, the Superannuation Guarantee Charge is currently set at 9 per cent of eligible gross wages—in this case, 9 per cent of $957.60. The first line links the superannuation calculation to the Superannuation Expense account. The second line links it to the Superannuation Liability account. Remember that the superannuation is not deducted from the employee's pay. It is calculated on the basis of eligible pay and is an additional expense for the employer.

▶ Click OK and tick the box to the left of Marcia Brown's name.

▶ Now click 'Stella, Simpson' to access Simpson Stella's payroll details (see figure 6.33, overleaf). In the Memo field, type in 'Simpson Stella Pay'. Simpson Stella worked 20 hours, so enter '20' beside the Base Hours, and his wages will be calculated automatically. Simpson Stella is a casual employee and so is not entitled to Annual Leave Pay or Personal Leave Pay. He is entitled to superannuation, but as his monthly gross wages are less than $450, he has not achieved the entitlement threshold and so will not receive any superannuation with this pay. Notice that at the top of the window the payment method and the account from which the pay will be paid are displayed. These items can be edited at this stage if necessary. Click OK and tick the box to the left of the Simpson Stella's name.

Figure 6.33: Pay Employee window: payroll details for Simpson Stella

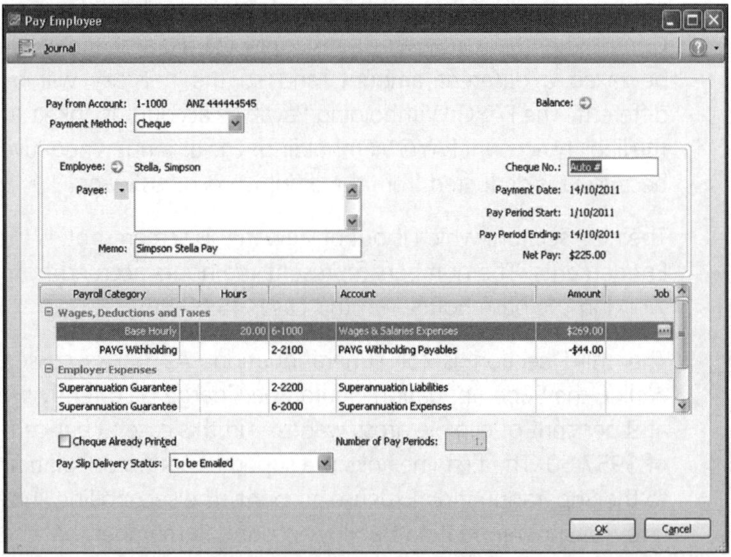

▶ As an aid to future searches, it's useful to enter the employee's name in the Memo field. Go to the pay information for Tania Jones (see exercise 6.4 on p. 235) and Rosemary Bostick (see exercise 6.3 on p. 234) and enter their names in the Memo field in the Pay Employee window ('Tania Jones Pay', 'Rosemary Bostick Pay'). Review their pay details and click OK. Tick the box to the left of the names Tania Jones and Rosemary Bostick and make sure that all employees have been selected.

As at the bottom of figure 6.31 (on p. 239), the Process Payroll: Employee Pays tab should say on the left '4 employees selected'.

▶ Click Record at the bottom of the Process Payroll: Employee Pays tab. An MYOB window will pop up to advise you that you are about to record four pays. Click OK.

▶ Once you have recorded the payroll, the next tab in
the Process Payroll wizard is the Process Payroll: Process
Payments tab (see figure 6.34). This window provides a
summary of the payment method used for the payroll
you have just processed. There is the option to print pay
cheques here. Try this for yourself and print them. Personally,
I usually skip this section, as I prefer to email pay advice to
employees. Once you have explored this window, click Next.

Figure 6.34: Process Payroll: Process Payments window

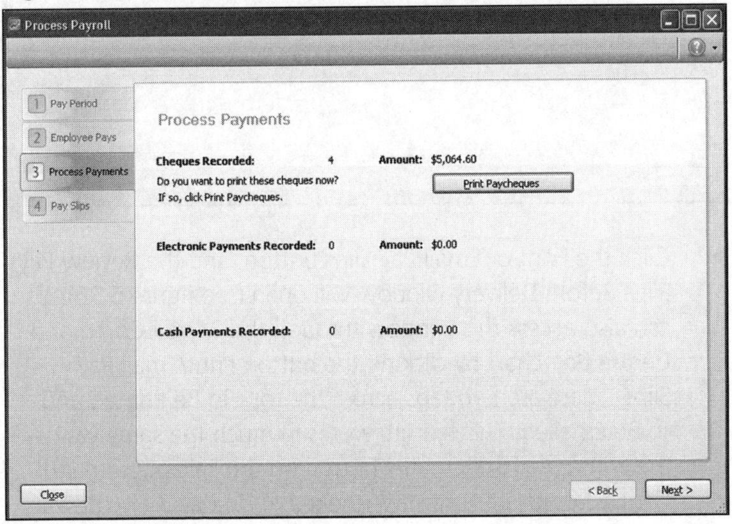

The next tab in the Process Payroll wizard takes you to the
Process Payroll: Pay Slips window (see figure 6.35, overleaf).
Pay Slips can be printed or emailed from here.

Figure 6.35: Process Payroll: Pay Slips window

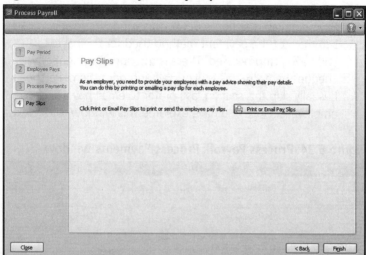

▶ Click the Print or Email Pay Slips button, and the Review Pay Slips Before Delivery window will open (see figure 6.36). You can also access this window through the Payroll Command Centre flowchart by clicking the button Print/Email Pay Slips. There are two tabs across the top: To Be Printed and To Be Emailed. This feature works in much the same way as the Print/Email Statements button on the Sales Command Centre flowchart, which we looked at on day 3. If you want to change the delivery method of the pay slip, double-click on a pay slip and then go to the Pay Slip Delivery Status field and change it accordingly. The Pay Slip Delivery Status field can be seen at bottom left in figure 6.33 (on p. 242).

Figure 6.36: Review Pay Slips Before Delivery window

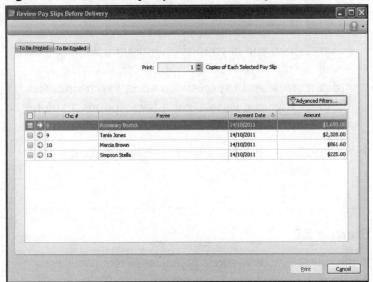

Customising pay slips

Pay slips can be customised by the inclusion of such things as company logos and branding. You will recall that we learned how to customise forms within the Sales Command Centre of MYOB AccountRight on day 3. I am frequently asked to remove the field Annual Salary on pay slips. Unfortunately, this field is on the pay slips by default and presents a misleading annual salary for part-time or casual workers.

▶ To access the payroll templates, click Setup →
Customise Forms → Pay Slips [or Paycheques] →
Customise. If you opt to customise the Paycheques
form, when you open the customisation window you
will see the Layout field at top centre. Click the drop-
down arrow and I suggest you select Paycheque. You
can choose from various pay advice options. Explore
them and choose what best suits your business.

▶ Click Close and then click Finish to complete the
Payroll process.

Exercise 6.6

In this exercise you will Process Payroll for all four employees.

Payment Date:	28 October 20XX
Pay period start:	15 October 20XX
Pay period end:	28 October 20XX

All employees are paid exactly the same pay as they were paid
the previous fortnight, including Simpson Stella, who is paid
for 20 hours' work. Once you have manually entered the hours
Simpson works, notice what this has done to his superannuation.
His superannuation may seem abnormally large. During the month
his earnings have exceeded the $450 superannuation threshold
and so he is entitled to superannuation on eligible earnings for the
entire month, not just for this pay period.

Processing annual and personal leave

We now need to run a third payroll for Green Apple Gym. During the past fortnight Tania has taken one day's annual leave, Rosemary has had a half-day's sick leave, and Simpson worked 7.6 hours. These events need to be recognised in the payroll system, as it has been set up to track both annual leave and personal leave.

Before we process the payroll, let's take a look at their accrued entitlements. Go to Reports → Payroll → Balance Summary to view the Entitlement Balance Summary Report (see figure 6.37).

Figure 6.37: Entitlement Balance Summary Report, July–November 2011

				Green Apple Gym	
Entitlement Balance [Summary]				1 Penny Lane, Orchard Way	
July 2011 To November 2011				ABN: 44 554 455 445	
				Email: green@applegym.com	
Entitlement	Opening Hours	Hours Accrued	Hours Taken	Available Hours	Value
Bostick, Rosemary		*None			
Annual Leave Accrual	0.00	11.69	0.00	11.69	$327.38
Personal Leave Accrual	0.00	5.85	0.00	5.85	$163.69
Total::	0.00	17.54	0.00	17.54	$491.06
Brown, Marcia		*None			
Annual Leave Accrual	0.00	7.02	0.00	7.02	$147.34
Personal Leave Accrual	0.00	3.51	0.00	3.51	$73.67
Total::	0.00	10.52	0.00	10.52	$221.00
Jones, Tania		*None			
Annual Leave Accrual	0.00	11.69	0.00	11.69	$467.68
Personal Leave Accrual	0.00	5.85	0.00	5.85	$233.84
Total::	0.00	17.54	0.00	17.54	$701.52

Notice that there are nil Opening Hours, because they are new employees. The hours have accrued from the two previous payrolls you processed. No hours have been taken, because no annual or personal leave has been processed in the payroll to date. The Available Hours for both Tania and Rosemary are the same, but the Value is different because their hourly rate is different. The Value column represents the hourly rate multiplied by the available hours.

Note, too, that if an employee leaves the business, the business is obliged to pay the employee for accrued annual leave but not for accrued personal leave. If you are a small business you should be conscious of this and encourage staff to take their holidays annually, so that you don't accrue a significant entitlements liability. Depending on the size of the business you may want to accrue annual and personal leave as a liability in your Balance Sheet. MYOB AccountRight does not automatically do this, you need to enter a manual journal entry to account for the accrual and adjust it periodically. Once an employee has been with a business for five years it is prudent to start accruing for Long Service Leave, recording it on their payslip and in the Balance Sheet.

Now process the following period for Green Apple Gym:

Payment date: 12 December 20XX

Pay period start: 29 November 20XX

Pay period end: 12 December 20XX

▶ In the Review Pay Slips Before Delivery window (see figure 6.36 on p. 245), click the zoom arrow beside Tania Jones. We need to recognise that Tania has taken one day's annual leave. Because she works a 38-hour week, this equates to 7.6 hours. Click the white zoom arrow beside Annual Leave Pay, and the Leave Tracking Information window opens (see figure 6.38).

Figure 6.38: Leave Tracking Information window

- In the Hours Taken field, enter 7.6. In both the Leave Started and Leave Finished fields, enter 29/11/20XX to indicate that Tania Jones has taken Monday 1 November as a personal leave day. In the Notes field, enter '1 day leave approved by Rosemary Bostick'. In real life, you can add any notes you like here or leave the field blank. Click OK.

- Notice that the Base Hourly amount automatically reduces by 7.6 to reflect the reduction in base hours worked that week. Click OK.

▶ Click the zoom arrow beside Rosemary Bostick. We need to recognise and record that Rosemary has taken a half-day as personal leave. A day is 7.6 hours, so this equates to 3.8 hours. This was calculated by dividing a 38-hour week by five days and then halving it. If in reality your work week was a different number of hours, say 40 hours, the daily and half-daily calculation would be different. Click the white zoom arrow beside Personal Leave Pay.

▶ In the Hours Taken field, enter 3.80. In both the Leave Started and Leave Finished fields, enter 7/12/20XX to indicate that Rosemary Bostick has taken Wednesday 7 December as a personal leave day. In this exercise we will leave the Notes field blank, however the field has space for 255 characters so you can leave a detailed reason for the absence if necessary. Click OK.

▶ Notice again that the Base Hours have automatically adjusted. If you are using an older version of MYOB, you will need to adjust the base hours manually. It is important to realise this otherwise you may be overpaying staff. Click OK.

▶ Remember to adjust Simpson Stella's pay by 7.6 hours.

▶ Select Record and process the payroll.

Now that you have processed an adjustment for entitlements, let's take a look at the Entitlements Balance Summary Report. Go to Reports → Payroll → Balance Summary to view the Entitlement Balance Summary Report (see figure 6.39). Notice that the figures in the Hours Taken column have been adjusted, and the Available Hours and Value columns have been reduced accordingly. Click Close.

Figure 6.39: Entitlement Balance Summary Report, July–December 2011

				Green Apple Gym
				1 Penny Lane,
Entitlement Balance [Summary]				Orchard Way
July 2011 To December 2011				ABN: 44 554 455 445
				Email: green@applegym.com

Entitlement	Opening Hours	Hours Accrued	Hours Taken	Available Hours	Value
Bostick, Rosemary			*None		
Annual Leave Accrual	0.00	17.54	0.00	17.54	$491.06
Personal Leave Accrual	0.00	8.77	3.80	4.97	$139.13
Total:	0.00	26.31	3.80	22.51	$630.20
Brown, Marcia			*None		
Annual Leave Accrual	0.00	10.52	0.00	10.52	$221.00
Personal Leave Accrual	0.00	5.26	0.00	5.26	$110.50
Total:	0.00	15.79	0.00	15.79	$331.51
Jones, Tania			*None		
Annual Leave Accrual	0.00	17.54	7.60	9.94	$397.52
Personal Leave Accrual	0.00	8.77	0.00	8.77	$350.76
Total:	0.00	26.31	7.60	18.71	$748.28

Review of Process Payroll

Now that you have processed three payrolls, it's useful to view the effect they have had on the accounts so that you have a thorough understanding of payroll.

Go to the Payroll Command Centre and click the Transaction Journal. Then select the Disbursements tab and select the period 1 October 20XX–30 November 20XX. You will see the journal entries for the employees' pays here. Look for Simpson Stella's first pay. Note that his superannuation has a nil value. Click Close.

Call up the Balance Sheet as at 31 December 20XX. In the Liabilities section you will see the Payroll Liabilities, consisting of PAYG Withholding and Superannuation Liabilities. The business currently owes $5560.32 (depending on the tax tables used), as shown in table 6.4.

Table 6.4: extract from Balance Sheet showing accrued Payroll Liabilities

Payroll liabilities	Amount
PAYG withholding	$3858.00
superannuation liabilities	$1702.32
Total PAYROLL LIABILITIES	$5560.32

Call up the Profit and Loss Statement for the period 1 October 20XX through to 31 December 20XX (see figure 6.40). In the Cost of Sales section you will see the account Wages COS, which represents the personal trainer wages. This cost is reflected in the Gross Profit figure. In the Expenses section you will see Wages and Salaries Expenses and Superannuation Expenses. This is reflected in the Operating Profit figure.

Figure 6.40: extract of Profit and Loss Statement for the period 1 October 20XX through to 31 December 20XX

			Green Apple Gym
Profit & Loss Statement			1 Penny Lane, Orchard Way
October 2011 To December 2011			ABN: 44 554 455 445
			Email: green@applegym.com
Income			
INVENTORY INCOME			
Equipment Income		$33.00	
Health Food Income		$6.00	
1 on 1 Fitness Class Income			$109.09
Group Training Income			$727.27
Total Income			$875.36
Cost Of Sales			
Fitness Accessories COGS			$654.55
INVENTORY COS			
Equipment COS		$68.18	
Health Food COS		$2.42	
Stock Write-Offs			$21.76
Wages COS			$11,992.80
Discount for Early Payment			-$13.64
Total Cost Of Sales			$12,726.07
Gross Profit			-$11,850.71
Expenses			
Wages & Salaries Expenses			$7,293.22
Office Stationary			$518.19
Bank Charges			$5.00
Postage			$45.45
Telephone Expense			$72.73
Superannuation Expenses			$1,702.32
Uniforms			$351.82
Rent			$909.10
Cleaning Expenses			$545.45
Total Expenses			$11,443.28
Other Expenses			
Net Profit/(Loss)			-$23,293.99

PAYG withholding

PAYG withholding payments are processed on the businesses Income Activity Statements (IAS) and Business Activity Statements (BAS). They can be paid monthly, quarterly or annually depending on how the business is registered to pay them with the ATO. It may be worth reiterating that PAYG withholding is not an expense of the business. The expense is the employees' wages and the PAYG withholding is withheld from their wages and remitted to the ATO. We will cover these on day 7.

Paying superannuation liability

The business is required to pay the employees' superannuation guarantee charge at least four times a year by the 28th day after the end of the BAS quarters: July–September, October–December, January–March, April–June.

Recently a free superannuation clearing house service was introduced for small businesses with fewer than 20 employees. Rather than pay the superannuation liability to individual superannuation funds, the business can pay the lump superannuation expense to the clearing house, and it does the rest. For more information visit: <www.medicareaustralia.gov. au/super/index.jsp>.

Green Apple Gym has not yet registered for the superannuation clearing house and needs to pay the superannuation fund directly.

▶   Click the Pay Liabilities button on the Payroll Command Centre, and the Pay Liabilities window opens (see figure 6.41, overleaf).

Figure 6.41: Pay Liabilities window

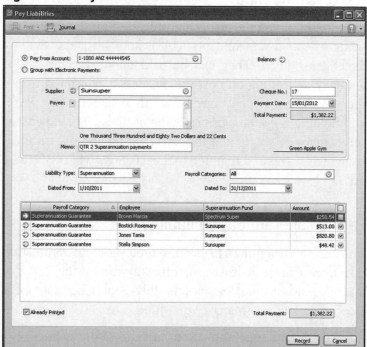

▶   In the Liability Type field, select Superannuation.

▶   In the Dated From field, enter 1/10/20XX. In the Dated
    To field, enter 31/12/20XX.

▶   Click the header of the Superannuation Fund column
    to sort the column. Tick all Sunsuper superannuation
    payments (the last three).

▶ Create a new card for the supplier Sunsuper, and then select the supplier Sunsuper.

▶ Click Edit, then Recap Transaction to view the transaction that you are about to record. Notice that it has picked up every individual superannuation payment.

▶ Record the transaction on 15 January the following year.

Exercise 6.7

Process the superannuation obligation for Spectrum Super for the second quarter, 1 October 20XX through to 31 December 20XX. You will need to create a Supplier Card for Spectrum Super. Date the transaction 15 January of the following year.

Note that PAYG withholding obligations can be paid in this way. You simply need to select Liability Type Tax and make the payment to the ATO.

Summary of day 6

Day 6 has introduced you to the Payroll Command Centre, payroll categories, Employee Cards, processing payroll, accruing entitlements and paying payroll liabilities. On our final day, day 7, we will go through the process of setting up a data file and a BAS template. You will learn how to use the Command Panel, the To Do List and the Company Data Auditor, and become familiar with the concepts of the payroll year and the financial year.

Day 7

The wrap

Key terms and concepts

▶ *Business activity statement (BAS):* a statement used by businesses registered for GST to report and pay a number of tax obligations, including GST, PAYG withholding and PAYG instalments. Business Activity Statements can be prepared on a monthly, quarterly or annual basis.

▶ *Instalment Activity Statement (IAS):* a statement used by businesses to report PAYG withholding to the ATO. **Instalment Activity Statements** can be prepared on a monthly or quarterly basis. If a business reports PAYG withholding monthly and a BAS is due for the month, an IAS is not required for that month. In this example, the business would submit an IAS in February and March and a BAS in April.

Introduction and overview

Finally, day 7 is here! Hurrah! How are you feeling? You have already achieved so much. You have now covered many of the basic areas of MYOB AccountRight software. You have set up a data file from scratch and explored the Banking, Sales and Purchases area. You have also set up employees and processed payroll. You have created inventory items and processes. Our task for today is to fill in a few gaps, to enhance some of the information you learned and practised on the previous days, and to set you up to confidently use your MYOB AccountRight software in the real world.

Using the Command Panel

First of all, it's time to take a closer look at the Command Panel. The Command Panel sits beneath the Flow Chart (see figure 7.1). It gives you access to various data-mining and analysis tools via the following buttons: To Do List, Find Transactions, Reports, and Business Insights. (Earlier versions of MYOB AccountRight have an Analysis button instead a Business Insights button.)

Notice that the buttons are split in two on the right-hand side. If you click the left side of the button, a new window relevant to the Command Centre you are currently working within opens. If you click the right side, a drop-down menu (actually it should be referred to as a drop-up menu due to the way it is configured) appears and you can select the specific area you wish to enter. Now that you have some data in your MYOB file, we can explore each of the four areas.

Figure 7.1: MYOB AccountRight home screen: Accounts Command Centre

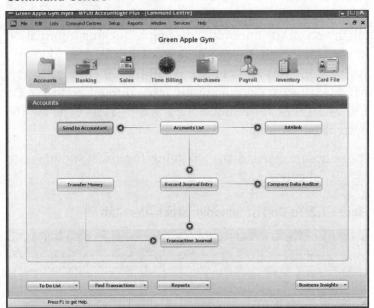

To Do List

Once you have started working within MYOB AccountRight, the To Do List provides a quick overview of the tasks that need to be done in MYOB, including attending to accounts receivable and accounts payable, following up on recurring transactions and low inventory alerts, and sending emails or making phone calls. It's a good practice to review the To Do List on a Monday morning to determine what needs to be done during the week, and you can then set priorities.

So how do we set up these 'feeds'? As an example, we will set up the To Do List to alert us if stock is running low and needs to be reordered. As we discussed on day 5, when you are setting up inventory, the Optional Restocking Information for the To Do List area on the Buying Details tab gives you the option of entering restocking information in the Minimum Level for Restocking Alert field. Once you've done this and completed all the other fields in this window, this data automatically feeds through to the To Do List and generates a Stock Alert when stock is below the designated threshold.

▶ Click the Stock Alerts tab in the To Do List window (see figure 7.2).

Figure 7.2: To Do List window: Stock Alert tab

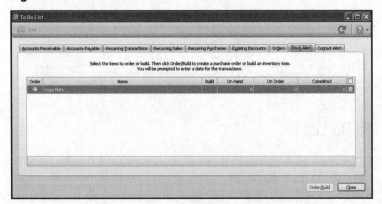

▶ The stock level for the Yoga Mats has fallen below the minimum threshold. To generate a purchase order, tick the check box on the right-hand side.

▶ Click the Order/Build button, and the Transaction Date window opens (see figure 7.3).

▶ Enter a date for the selected transaction, 30/11/20XX, and click OK.

Figure 7.3: Transaction Date window

▶ The Stock Alert clears from the To Do List Window and will generate a purchase order automatically. To verify this:

▶ Click the Close button.

▶ Select the Purchase Command Centre.

▶ Select the Purchase Register button, and ensure that the date range includes 30/11/20XX.

▶ Click the Orders tab and you will see the new purchase order. Click on the white zoom arrow to view the details.

Find Transactions

When you are investigating an issue—for example, the bank reconciliation won't balance—you usually know something about the transaction. The Find Transactions area allows you to search transactions within MYOB using a wide range of criteria. (As an MYOB Certified Consultant who resolves problems, I spend a lot of time here.)

For example, let's suppose we are looking for a $500 transaction that occurred in November.

▶ Click the Find Transactions button, and the Find Transactions window opens (see figure 7.4).

Turbo tip

Try hitting [Ctrl-Y] and see how you go...

Figure 7.4: Find Transactions window

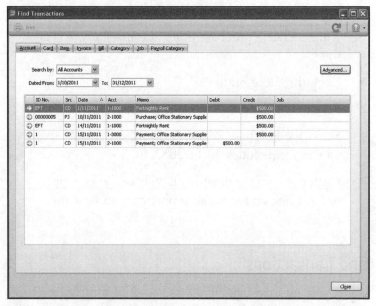

▶ Click the Account tab of the Find Transactions window.

▶ Click the Advanced tab at top right and the Advanced Filters window opens (see figure 7.5).

Figure 7.5: Advanced Filters window

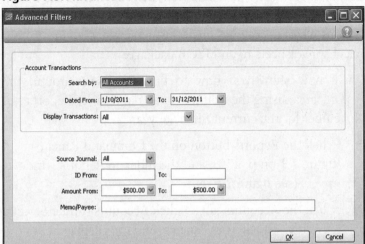

▶ The default 'Search by' option is All Accounts. This is what we want here.

▶ The default Dated From option is 1 November through to 30 November, but you can choose to search a wider date range if you wish.

▶ Enter $500 in the Amount From and To fields.

▶ All transactions that include $500 will appear in the Find Transactions window (see figure 7.4).

▶ You can use the drill-down arrow to explore the detail of the transactions returned.

▶ Once you have found the required transaction, click the Close button.

Reports

The Reports area gives you easy access to hundreds of accounting reports that you can use to help you make business decisions. You can choose to view, print or export them, and they can all be customised. This facility is one of the main reasons why I encourage small business owners to move from Excel spreadsheets to an MYOB package.

I will now show you how to find your way around the Reports area, using the example of a Trial Balance Report as of November for the current financial year.

▶ Click the Reports button on the Command Panel (see figure 7.1 on p. 259), and the Index to Reports window opens (see figure 7.6).

▶ Click the Accounts tab → click Accounts (under Select Report) → click Trial Balance, and the Display Report options appear.

Figure 7.6: Index to Reports window

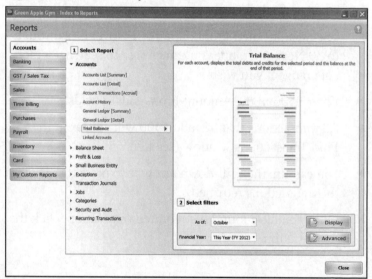

At the top of the screen you will see a short description of each report. The Trial Balance reproduced here (corresponding to figure 7.7) displays the total debits and credits for the selected period and the balance at the end of that period for each account.

▶ Enter the report criteria at bottom left of the Display Report panel. In our example, we select 'November' in the 'As of' field and 'This Year (FY20XX)' in the Financial Year field.

▶ Click the Display button, and the Trial Balance Report is displayed. An extract is shown in figure 7.7, as the report is too long to display here.

Figure 7.7: Trial Balance Report (extract)

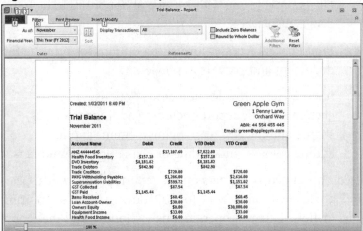

Along the top of the Trial Balance report you will see two icons and a drop-down arrow, which accesses the following options:

▶ *Save Reports As* allows the user to customise, rename and redescribe the report, and to save it under the My Custom Report tab.

▶ *Print Report* is self-explanatory.

▶ *Customise Quick Access Toolbar* switches the toolbar to above or below the ribbon.

Below the icons are four tabs:

▶ *File* gives you the options of exporting the report in various formats, saving the report (once you have customised it) or printing the report.

▶ *Filters* provide you with a range of options as to how the data is displayed.

▶ *Print Preview* accesses formatting options for printing the document and provides a preview.

▶ *Insert/Modify* provides numerous options for customising the report, including adding text boxes, shapes and images; rearranging columns and fields; adding colours; and adding or changing page numbers.

If you hover across the data on the report, a hand will appear, and a click will allow you to drill down to the supporting information. This will open in a new window, and the report window remains open.

The Trial Balance is quite a simple report. Take some time to explore other reports. The data within MYOB can be accessed from many different angles, and you need to identify what information you need to make business decisions and to establish which reports will provide it. Also take some time to explore the many options MYOB provides for customising your reports, and try them out for yourself. (I especially like using Row Shading, combined with a subtle Page Colour.)

▶ To close the Trial Balance report, click the minimise button and click Close.

Business Insights

Business Insights is a new feature of MYOB AccountRight software (introduced in AccountRight version 19 in 2010). It is accessed on the right-hand side of the Command Panel and operates like a dashboard for business finances—a user-friendly overview of important financial information. Providing as it does interactive tables and graphs, with the option of further analysis, it's an important area, even for the business owner who does not like numbers!

To access the Business Insights dashboard, go to the Accounts Command Centre, click the Business Insights button and the Business Insights window opens (see figure 7.8).

Figure 7.8: Business Insights window

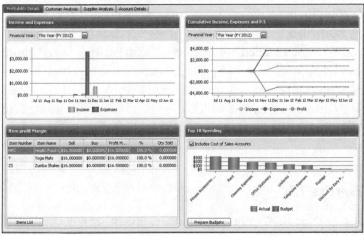

You will see four tabs across the top: Profitability Details, Customer Analysis, Supplier Analysis and Account Details.

Profitability Details is divided into four sections: 'Income and Expenses', Cumulative Income, Expenses and P/L', 'Item profit margin' and 'Top 10 Spending'.

Customer Analysis is divided into four sections: 'Customers who owe me money', 'Top 10 customers by YTD sales value', 'Aged receivables' and 'Customer sales history'.

The Supplier Analysis is divided into four sections: 'Suppliers I need to pay', 'Top 10 suppliers by YTD purchases value', 'Aged payables' and 'Supplier purchase history'.

The Account Details is divided into three sections: 'Bank Account Credit Cards', 'Total Liabilities' and 'Total Assets'

To close the Business Insights dashboard, click Close.

Analysis

The Business Insights feature replaced the Analysis button found on the Command Panel of earlier versions of MYOB AccountRight software. As you may be using an earlier version, it's worth mentioning that the Analysis Selection window enables you to view detailed information about Balance Sheet, Profit and Loss, Jobs, Cash Flow, Sales, Receivables, Payables, Payroll and Inventory. Not all options are available in all packages. The Customer Analysis window is one of my favourite areas in MYOB, as it allows me to quickly see who owes money.

Exercise 7.1

This exercise shows you how to use reports to identify clients with outstanding debts.

- ▸ Go to the To Do List and click the Accounts Receivable tab.

- ▸ Locate and view the Aged Receivables Summary Report for November.

- ▸ Go to the Business Insights dashboard and view the 'Customers who owe me money' table. With this information, you could follow up on debt collection. For our purposes, however, click Close.

Setting up MYOB AccountRight software

When you start using MYOB, I hope you will be able to work on a data file that is set up correctly. That will make your life much easier. If you need to set up a data file from scratch, I strongly advise you to work through the whole book first so that you understand the basic processes and know what you are aiming for. You have no doubt heard that MYOB is easy to use, and that is probably one of the reasons why you chose it for your business, but you need to have some practical experience of the software before you attempt to set up a data file for your own business.

Day-to-day use of MYOB AccountRight software

You are now in a position to confidently use MYOB within a real-life business environment. From my own experience over many years of setting up hundreds of businesses to use MYOB software, I recommend that you review your own business processes to take full advantage of what MYOB AccountRight offers. It's also useful to prepare a tax calendar for your business showing the relevant lodgment and payment dates. The ATO <www.ato.gov.au> has a free tool on its website to help businesses create a customised tax calendar.

Checklists are very useful and can simply be an organised 'to do' list of the tasks within the accounts department and within MYOB AccountRight that need to be completed on a daily, weekly, monthly, quarterly and annual basis. Comprehensive customisable checklists are available for download at <www.learnMYOBin7days.com>. A typical quarterly checklist for a small business is shown in figure 7.9.

Not everything listed on this checklist will be relevant to your business. If you don't have inventory, for example, any procedures related stock control should be deleted. Your checklists will evolve with the business, and you should review them periodically.

Figure 7.9: typical quarterly checklist for a small business

		Quarter:
		Process date:
Step	*Procedure*	✓
Step 1	Separate paperwork into relevant stacks: Accounts Payable, Accounts Receivable, Bank, Inventory etc.	
Step 2	Enter Accounts Payable (supplier bills)/Reconcile Accounts Payable	
Step 3	Enter Accounts Receivable/Reconcile Accounts Receivable	
Step 4	Review inventory requirements/Reconcile Inventory	

Step	Procedure	✓
Step 5	Update the cash flow.	
Step 6	Reconcile • Bank Account • Credit Card Account • Trade Debtors • Trade Creditors • GST • PAYG Withholding • Superannuation Print reconciliations and file with paper statement. Print a second copy to PDF and store in Finances directory.	
Step 7	Calculate superannuation for subcontractors who are listed as suppliers and prepare payment.	
Step 8	Process electronic payments and upload bank file (.aba) file for authorisation OR print report and advise supervisor when ready for authorisation.	
Step 9	Fax or email remittance advices to suppliers.	
Step 10	Communicate with overdue Accounts Receivable. Analyse who is unlikely to pay and follow debt collection procedures.	
Step 11	Complaints follow-up; stock return follow-up	
Step 12	Stock levels – is there enough stock for upcoming promotions/projected sales?	
Step 13	Customer credit application processing and follow-up	
Step 15	Review GST and Payroll reports for preparation of BAS.	
Step 16	Run Company Data Auditor.	
Step 17	Account for any private usage through a journal entry.	
Step 18	Review hire, purchase and lease payments.	

Figure 7.9: *(cont'd)*

Step	Procedure	✓
Step 19	Review purchase of capital acquisitions.	
Step 20	Print profit and loss and balance sheet; check that balances are reasonable, e.g. • Petty cash • Cash drawer • Undeposited funds account • Historical balancing account	
Step 21	Prepare BAS using BASLink.	
Step 22	Print reports: • Profit and loss for month vs budget • Profit and loss YTD vs. budget • Balance sheet • AR reconciliation • AP reconciliation • Customer sales • Item sales • Bank reconciliation • Cash flow	
Step 23	Back up company file, label it QUARTER# BACKUP and maintain one in the standard file area, and store in secure area according to back-up procedures.	
Step 24	Lock the period that has been finalised.	
Completed by _____		
Signed_____		

As you can see from this checklist, there are still some gaps we need to fill in. You have yet to learn how use the Company Data Auditor and how to set up a BAS or IAS template. We will cover these and then run through a brief summary of the tasks that need to be done at the end of the payroll year and the financial year. We will finish off with 12 keys to using your AccountRight software efficiently and effectively.

Company Data Auditor

The Company Data Auditor is a tool that provides a high-level integrity check of data within MYOB. I recommend that you work through the Company Data Auditor on a regular basis, perhaps every Friday afternoon, and before completing a BAS/IAS. When I visit clients for the first time, the first aspect of MYOB I look at is their Company Data Auditor. It allows me to review many aspects of the data file and 'red flags' issues that may require closer inspection.

Go to the Accounts Command Centre and click the Company Data Auditor button, and the window will open at the Company File Overview tab (see figure 7.10).

Figure 7.10: Company Data Auditor: Company File Overview window

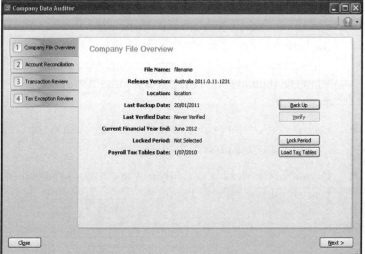

The first three items are self-explanatory. The others may need some explanation.

▶ *Last Backup Date.* Backing up is a process of compressing and saving a zipped file. The back-ups should be saved to a finance directory, not the default c:\ directory. If the computer system for your business is set up to automatically back up all files at the end of each day, it may not be necessary to back up the individual MYOB file.

▶ *Last Verified Date.* Verification is a process of scanning both the transactions and the computer code of the MYOB data file and checking for inconsistencies. This should be done on a regular basis. If a verification issue is highlighted, try optimising the file. If the issue persists, you may need to contact MYOB Australia directly.

▶ *Current Financial Year End.* If the field does not reflect the current financial year, previous financial years will need to be closed off. This is dependent on your tax accountant producing annual financial statements and the business or the accountant entering the year-end adjustments in the MYOB AccountRight data file to align the data file with the tax accountant's financial statements.

▶ *Locked Period.* Data prior to this date has been closed off, avoiding any unwanted changes.

▶ *Payroll Tax Tables Date.* 1 July of the current financial year should be reflected here.

Now click the Next button to open the Account Reconciliation
Review window (see figure 7.11).

**Figure 7.11: Company Data Auditor: Account Reconciliation
Review window**

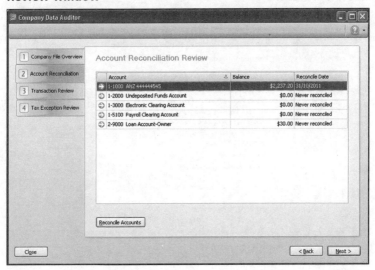

This window gives you an overview of reconciled accounts.
Only accounts that are Bank or Credit Card type will appear
here. You should check that the Reconcile Dates are recent,
and if you are preparing an IAS/BAS return, you need to check
that they were reconciled to at least the last date of the period.
If they are labelled 'Never reconciled' and the balance is not
zero, this warrants further investigation.

Click the Next button to open the Transaction Review window (see figure 7.12).

Figure 7.12: Company Data Auditor: Transaction Review window

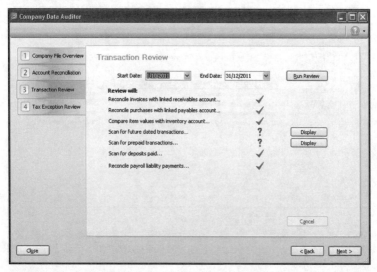

In this window and the Tax Exception Review window you need to choose a start date and an end date for the period in review. If you were preparing an IAS/BAS, the period would obviously be the period the IAS/BAS covers.

In this example, the second quarter of the BAS period has been selected (1 October to 31 December). Enter the period and click Run Review, and the Company Data Auditor processes the data and returns a red question mark and a Display button, which accesses a report highlighting transactional issues. Note that it's a red question mark, not a cross. It doesn't mean that something is wrong; it's just alerting you to the fact that there may be an issue. Likewise, the tick means that the data is presented in a correct manner, not that it's correct — the data may still contain errors or be fraudulent.

Click the Next button to open the Tax Exception Review window (see figure 7.13).

Figure 7.13: Company Data Auditor: Tax Exception Review window

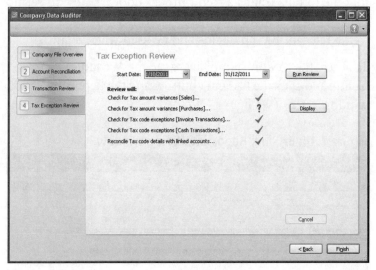

Enter the required period and click Run Review. The Tax Exception Review will highlight transactions where the tax code entered is different from the default tax code. There may be perfectly legitimate reasons for any differences; for example, office supplies may include a GST-free purchase of essential food items, and the review would highlight this difference. Alternatively, it may be that an account code was created but the relevant tax code was not assigned. When this is corrected and the review is rerun, the item will no longer be listed as containing a discrepancy.

Click the Finish button, and when asked if you would like to print a summary report click the Yes button and file the report.

BASlink

One of the many benefits of using MYOB is the time you save processing BAS. You were introduced to tax codes on day 1. You already know how to allocate default tax codes to account codes and then use the tax codes on transactions. You also know how to check them via the Company Data Auditor. Now it's time to take things a step further and learn how to set up BAS and IAS templates to enable information to filter through to the relevant BASlink fields and be used when required.

To access the IAS/BAS templates, go to the Accounts Command Centre and click the BASLink button, and the Reporting Period window opens (see figure 7.14).

Figure 7.14: BASlink Reporting Period window

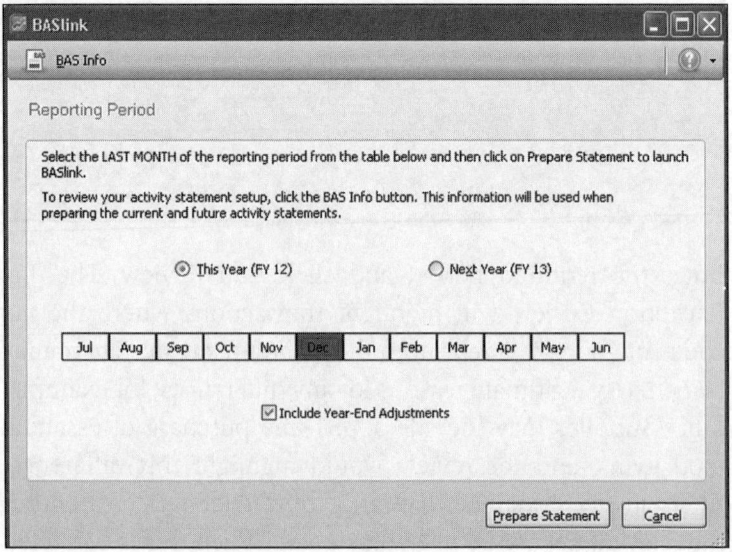

Click the BAS Info button at top left (bottom left in older versions of the software) to access the BAS Information: Set Up Activity Statement window (see figure 7.15 on p. 280).

The set-up process involves selecting the options that apply to your business from a list provided by the ATO. The available options for various business taxes and the list of responses you are required to select from are shown in table 7.1.

How you set up the business's BAS template will depend on how the business is registered with the ATO. The easiest way to determine this is to look at a recent BAS/IAS. If you don't have a copy, ask your accountant or bookkeeper for one. If none is available, you will need to contact the ATO to find out how the business registered with the ATO.

Table 7.1: complete list of ATO business tax options (data accessed in Set Up Activity Statement window)

Goods and services tax	
GST reporting frequency	Monthly, quarterly, annually, not registered
GST accounting basis	Non cash (accruals), cash
GST option	Option 1, option 2, option 3
GST instalment amount	$ (only for option 3)
What is the calculation method?	Accounts, calculation worksheet
I use the simplified accounting method	Yes, no
I claim fuel tax credits	Yes, no
PAYG instalments	
Instalment reporting frequency	Quarterly, not registered
Instalment accounting basis	Non cash (accruals), cash
Instalment option	Option 1, option 2
PAYG instalment amount/rate	Option 1: $, option 2: %
PAYG withholding	
Withholding reporting frequency	Not registered, monthly (medium withholder), quarterly (small withholder)
WET/LCT/FBT	
I have FBT, WET or LCT obligations	Yes, no

Complete the information as shown in the Set Up Activity Statement window (see figure 7.15), and then click OK to return to the Reporting Period window (see figure 7.14 on p. 278).

Figure 7.15: BAS Information: Set Up Activity Statement window

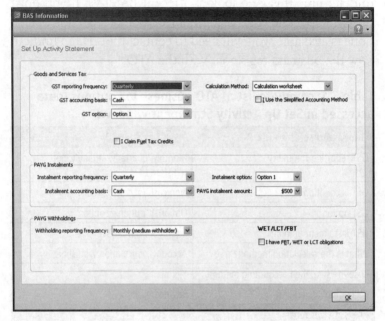

In the Reporting Period window, select 'This Year (FY XX)' and click 'Dec' to select December as the last month of the reporting period.

Click the Prepare Statement button and then click OK, and the BAS template opens. There is an easy way to determine if the BASlink template has been set up correctly. Click on the second tab across the top of the Front Sheet. In the top right-hand corner you should see a letter. This should be the same letter you see on the BAS/IAS form you received in the mail from the ATO. There are a number of different BAS templates. If the letters do not match, you will need to go back to the Set Up Activity Statement window and review the options you selected.

The BAS template looks almost identical to the BAS form you received in the mail, even down to the colour. There are three sheets, labelled as follows: GST worksheet, Front Sheet and Back Sheet.

Click the GST worksheet tab and we will work through an example to show you how to set it up. By linking the GST worksheet (see figure 7.16) to the relevant tax code, information will automatically fill out the BAS fields.

Figure 7.16: GST worksheet for BAS

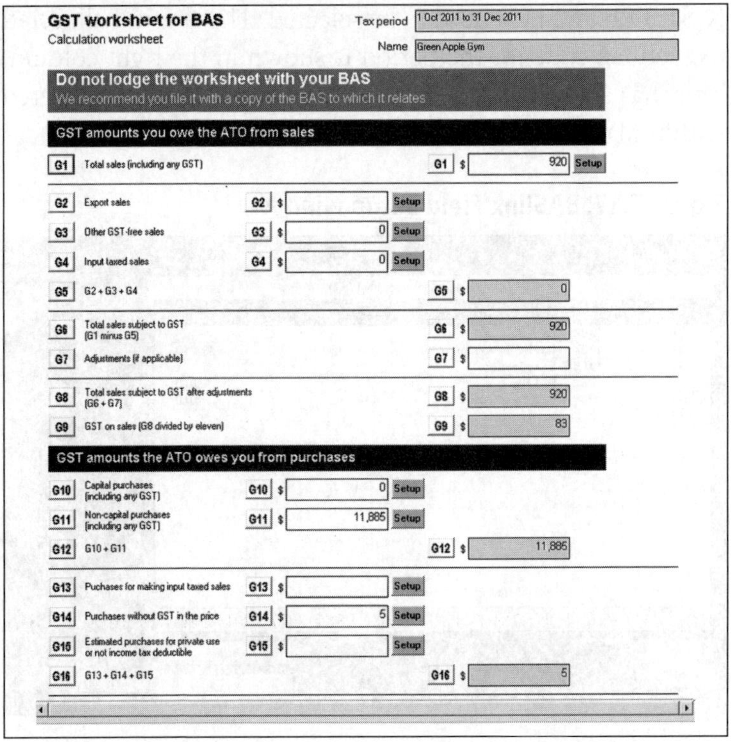

GST worksheet for BAS
Calculation worksheet

Tax period: 1 Oct 2011 to 31 Dec 2011
Name: Green Apple Gym

Do not lodge the worksheet with your BAS
We recommend you file it with a copy of the BAS to which it relates

GST amounts you owe the ATO from sales

G1	Total sales (including any GST)		G1 $ 920 Setup
G2	Export sales	G2 $ Setup	
G3	Other GST-free sales	G3 $ 0 Setup	
G4	Input taxed sales	G4 $ 0 Setup	
G5	G2 + G3 + G4		G5 $ 0
G6	Total sales subject to GST (G1 minus G5)		G6 $ 920
G7	Adjustments (if applicable)		G7 $
G8	Total sales subject to GST after adjustments (G6 + G7)		G8 $ 920
G9	GST on sales (G8 divided by eleven)		G9 $ 83

GST amounts the ATO owes you from purchases

G10	Capital purchases (including any GST)	G10 $ 0 Setup	
G11	Non-capital purchases (including any GST)	G11 $ 11,885 Setup	
G12	G10 + G11		G12 $ 11,885
G13	Purchases for making input taxed sales	G13 $ Setup	
G14	Purchases without GST in the price	G14 $ 5 Setup	
G15	Estimated purchases for private use or not income tax deductible	G15 $ Setup	
G16	G13 + G14 + G15		G16 $ 5

The tax period is shown at top right. Before you start, always check that this is the correct period.

On the first line, Total Sales (including any GST), there are three buttons. The two G1 buttons perform the same function; click either and a BASlink Help window opens, with detailed information about what should and should not be included at G1.

Beneath G1 you will see the following: 'G2 Export sales', 'G3 Other GST-free sales' and 'G4 Input taxed sales'. These are detailed subgroups that are included in the 'G1 Total sales (including any GST)' figure. Armed with this information, click the Setup button, and the Field Setup window opens (see figure 7.17). The three tax codes to be included at G1 (GST, FRE and ITS) need to be selected. The amount allocated to each tax code for the period is shown in the right column. This has automatically fed through from the date entered within MYOB.

Figure 7.17: BASlink Field Setup window

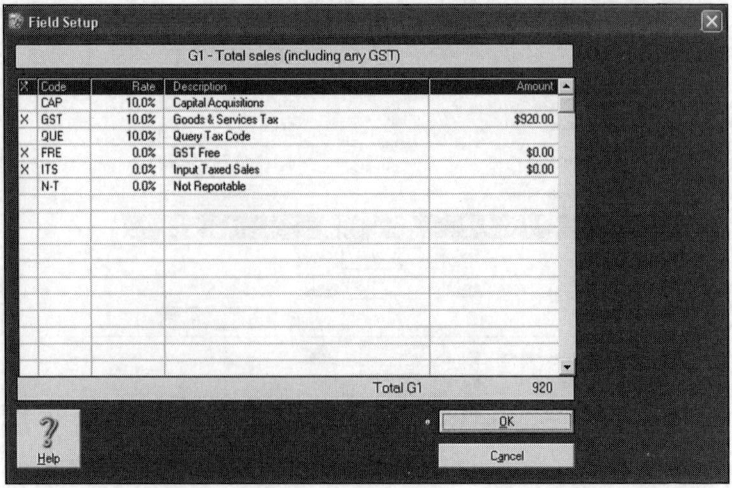

Click GST (Goods and Services Tax), and the amount column will fill with $920.

Click FRE (GST free), and the BASlink Setup Assistant window will open (see figure 7.18). As well as being reflected at 'G1 Total sales (including any GST)', the tax code FRE (GST Free) is allocated to G3 ('Other GST-free sales'). Click OK.

Figure 7.18: BASlink Setup Assistant window

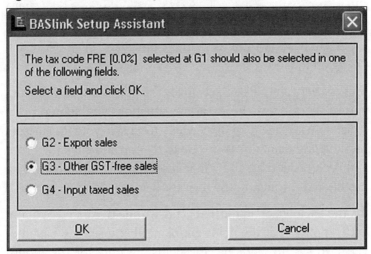

Click ITS, and once again the BASlink Setup Assistant window will open. Select 'G4-Input taxed sales'. The individual amount of input taxed sales is detailed at G$ and totalled into G1. Click OK.

As you scroll down the GST worksheet for BAS (see figure 7.16 on p. 281), you will notice a number of grey boxes. These fields cannot be altered and will auto-fill.

You should never enter an adjustment at the blank G7 or G18 fields unless directly advised to do so by the ATO.

At G10, click the grey Setup button and then select CAP (Capital acquisitions) and click ok.

At G11, click the grey setup button and click GST, then click FRE. The BASlink Setup Assistant window opens. Select G14 (Purchases without GST in the price) and click OK.

Click NRG ('Not registered for GST' formerly known as GNR) and the BASlink Setup Assistant window opens again. Select G14 (Purchases without GST in the price) and click OK. Click OK again to close.

This is a very simple BAS set-up for the purpose of introducing you to the process. In a real-life situation, you should get a registered tax agent or BAS agent to check your businesses BASlink and data file set-up. Go to the top and click the Front and Back Sheet tabs, and you will see that the underlying data has filtered through to the relevant fields.

On the Back Sheet, in the 'PAYG tax withheld' panel (see figure 7.19), notice that the fields are blank, because they have not yet been set up, and that the fields are only for the month of December. You will recall from the BAS Information: Set Up Activity Statement window (see figure 7.15 on p. 280) that we opted for PAYG withholding to be reported monthly. Therefore, only a month of PAYG withholding will be remitted with this BAS statement.

Figure 7.19: Back Sheet of BAS statement: PAYG tax withheld panel

PAYG tax withheld			
for the MONTH from 1 Dec 2011 to 31 Dec 2011			
Total salary, wages and other payments	**W1** $	6,227	Setup
Amounts withheld from payments shown at W1	**W2** $	1,286	Setup
Amounts withheld where no ABN is quoted	**W4** $		Setup
Other amounts withheld (excluding any amount shown at W2 or W4)	**W3** $		Setup
Total amounts withheld (W2 + W3 + W4) **Write at 4 in summary below**	**W5** $	1,286	

At W1, click Setup and then select All.

At W2, click Setup and then select PAYG Withholding.

If a business does not declare its ABN on its invoice, part of the payment due has to be retained and declared at W4. Other PAYG tax amounts that the business may withhold—for example, when an investor does not declare his or her tax file number—are declared at W3.

On the Menu Bar, click Reports → Exception Report to highlight any amounts that erroneously may not have been included in the BAS template. Amounts allocated to tax codes such as N-T (not reportable) should be in this report and not in the BAS Report. All tax-related transactions should appear in the BAS Report, and all non-tax transactions, which are therefore not reportable, should appear in the Exception Report.

Now click the large, square Transaction button at bottom left. Click No, then No again, and a Spend Money window opens, detailing how the BAS payment has been split across several different accounts. The BAS should not simply be applied to one general ledger account such as GST Paid. It should be split across GST Paid, GST Received, PAYG Withholding and other accounts that have recorded a tax liability, and thus should reflect the payment of the tax liability.

The transaction does not automatically record. You need to print the completed statement. You can then either enter the information on the ATO's BAS form or lodge an electronic version via the Business portal found on the ATO website.

Click Save Setup and Exit, click Yes, click Save, and you will drop back to the BASlink Reporting Period window (see figure 7.14 on p. 278). Well done!

Now that we have set up a BAS template, the necessary fields for the IAS statement will already be selected. Many businesses will never have to deal with an IAS, which only applies to businesses that report to the ATO on a monthly basis.

All that remains now is for us to generate the IAS. This is a very simple process. In the Reporting Period window, select November and click Prepare Statement, and the business's IAS statement will open. You will see that the statement is pre-filled from the BAS template set-up.

Click Save Setup and Exit, click Yes, then click Save, and finally click Cancel. We're done!

Financial year versus payroll year

The tasks that have to be done at the end of the financial year and the end of the payroll year are beyond the scope of this book, but it's important that you understand the concepts of financial year and payroll year and how they differ.

The financial year is an accounting concept, a period that typically runs for 12 months from 1 July through to 30 June. Organisations with foreign links, not-for-profit organisations and some other organisations may use a different period, such as the calendar year. The relevant financial year can be set up when the MYOB data file is initially created. The ATO assesses a business's tax obligations on the basis of its financial year, and this is also the period the business uses for budgeting and planning purposes.

Within MYOB AccountRight, the Payroll Year runs completely separately from the Financial Year. The Payroll Year must run from 1 July through to 30 June. Once the last payroll for the year has been run, the business needs to review the year's payroll and prepare Payment Summaries. It's a legal requirement that payment summaries be issued to employees by 14 July each year. Once the Payment Summaries have been prepared, the Payroll Year must be closed off. (Older versions of MYOB use the term 'rolled over'.) Payroll cannot be processed from 1 July onwards until this has been done. Once a Payroll Year has been closed off, payroll within that year cannot be edited and the process cannot be undone. This is a very hectic time of the year for a business, and it's wise to be prepared for what needs to be done.

12 keys to staying in tiptop form

The following insights will help you to use MYOB AccountRight efficiently and effectively, so that you can produce timely financial reports and comply with your tax obligations.

1 Ensure that your MYOB software is set up properly

It's important to have your data file set up properly by someone who knows what they are doing, such as your accountant or a suitably qualified business consultant. This small investment will give your business a strong foundation and bring a big return.

2 Invest in adequate training

Investing in expert training in the use of MYOB AccountRight will empower you to manage your business.

The following are some useful resources:

▶ <www.learnMYOBin7days.com>

▶ <www.MYOB.com.au/supportnotes>

▶ *Learn Bookkeeping in 7 Days* by Rod Caldwell (published by Wrightbooks 2010).

3 Ensure that all accounts are reconciled

You should reconcile all accounts that you receive statements for, such as bank accounts, credit card accounts and term deposits. Once you have completed the reconciliation, print the reconciliation statement and staple it to the front of the statements reconciled. You can also store a PDF in the Finance directory.

We explored Bank Reconciliations on day 2 when we looked at the Banking Command Centre, and now that we have some data in the data file, it's a good opportunity to run through a bank reconciliation exercise.

Exercise 7.2

Bank Reconciliations: a worked example

▶ Go to the Banking Command Centre and click the Reconcile Accounts button, and the Reconcile Accounts window opens (see figure 7.20).

Figure 7.20: Reconcile Accounts window

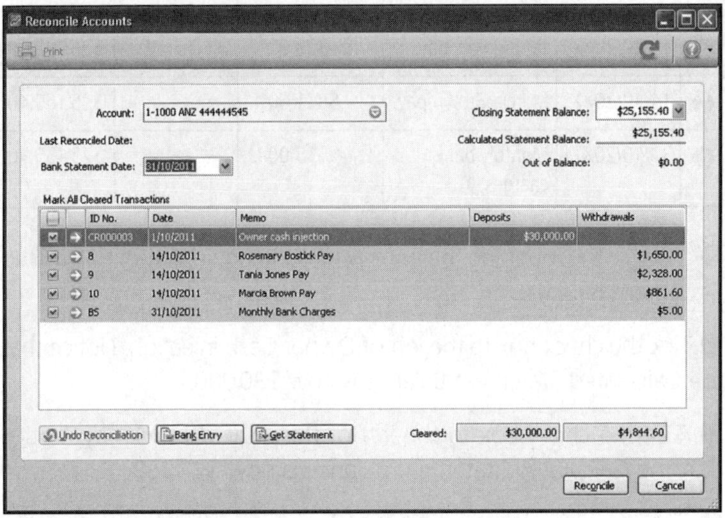

▶ In the Account field, select '1-1000 ANZ Bank Account'.

▶ Tab through to the Closing Statement Balance field and enter $25510.40. This amount would be sourced from the Bank Statement.

▶ Tab through to the Bank Statement Date and enter 31/10/20XX.

▶ You now need to compare the bank statement (see table 7.2) with the account being reconciled within MYOB.

Table 7.2: extract from ANZ bank statement for Green Apple Gym, 1/10/20XX to 31/10/20XX

	Date	Transaction details	Withdrawals	Deposits	Balance
❶	01/10/20XX	Opening balance			$0.00
❷	01/10/20XX	Owner cash injection		$30,000.00	$30 000.00
❸	14/10/20XX	Rosemary Bostick pay	$1 650.00		$28 350.00
❹	14/10/20XX	Tania Jones pay	$2 328.00		$26 022.00
❺	14/10/20XX	Marcia Brown pay	$861.60		$25 160.40
❻	31/10/20XX	Monthly bank charges	$5.00		$25 155.40

❶ This is the opening balance; check it against the Calculated Statement Balance.

❷ Tick the check box to the left of Owner Cash injection. Notice that the Calculated Statement Balance is now $30 000.

❸ Tick the check box to the left of Rosemary Bostick Pay. Notice that the Calculated Statement Balance is now $28 350.

❹ Tick the check box to the left of Tania Jones Pay. Notice that the Calculated Statement Balance is now $26 022.

❺ Tick the check box to the left of Marcia Brown Pay. Notice that the Calculated Statement Balance is now $25 160.40.

I have spelt out the changes in the calculated statement balance in detail here to make the point that you will process your reconciliations faster if you work through them methodically in date order and deal with issues as they arise.

❻ The bank statement shows that there has been a $5 bank charge, but note that there is no corresponding transaction in your MYOB data file. This is a typical scenario. The bank statement is a source document and is where you will first discover the existence of bank charges. These bank charges need to be entered during the reconciliation process.

▶ Use Spend Money to record monthly bank charges on 31/10/XX (Account Code 6-1110, Tax Code FRE). Return to the Reconcile Accounts window. You may need to click the green arrow at top right to refresh the window.

▶ Tick the check box to the left of Monthly Bank Charges. Notice that the Calculated Statement Balance is now $25 155.40 and that the Out of Balance field at top right is zero. Click the Reconcile button, click the Print Report button, and then click the Reconcile button and click the Reconcile button again. The bank statement has now been reconciled with the MYOB data.

4 Never post a transaction directly to a control account

A control account is a general ledger account that summarises a group of detailed individual accounts. For example, Trade Debtors is the control account that summarises accounts receivable. Trade Creditors, Inventory, GST Collected and GST Paid are other examples of control accounts.

Transactions should almost never be posted directly to a control account. Identify the individual account the transaction affects and process it through that account. (There are limited exceptions to this rule.)

5 Set up your linked accounts correctly and then don't tamper with them

Linked accounts need to be set up correctly on day one and then they should be left alone. Make sure that you don't accidentally change the name of a linked account or amend the links, and don't change any links unless you are very confident that you know what you are doing.

6 Restrict access to closed periods by utilising Locked Periods

Once you have prepared your BAS or IAS and submitted it to the ATO, prevent adjustments being made to any figures from previous periods by locking down the period just past.

If any adjustments are necessary, they need to be made in the current period and will be reflected in the subsequent BAS or IAS. If adjustments are made in earlier periods, the GST reports for the present period will not reflect them and consequently your GST claims or payments may be incorrect.

7 Establish a useful and relevant Chart of Accounts

The Chart of Accounts is the backbone of your business management reporting system, and all transactions should be posted to the selected general ledger lines. It's your information, so you need to include accounts that are relevant to your business while ensuring that you are not creating unnecessary accounts. On day 2, when we explored the Banking Command Centre, you learned how to create, edit and delete accounts. It's also possible to combine accounts and to group accounts in different levels by utilising header and details accounts.

Combining general ledger accounts is an alternative option to deleting an account. Historical information is retained in the combined account. To keep your reports simple and manageable I would aim to have the minimum number of general ledger lines that you can get by with rather than overwhelm the user with detail.

Before you attempt to combine accounts, check that:

▶   they are detail, not header, accounts

▶   they are not linked to anything

▶   they are the same type of account.

To see how this works, we will combine '4-1100 Fitness Equipment Sales' with the account '4-1410 Equipment Income' and then delete '4-1100'.

▶   Go to the Accounts Command Centre (see figure 7.1 on p. 259) and click Accounts List, and the Accounts List window opens.

▶   Find '4-1410 Equipment Income' and click it once. Then click the Combine Accounts button at bottom left of the Accounts List, and the Combine Accounts Window will open (see figure 7.21, overleaf).

Figure 7.21: Accounts List: Combine Accounts window

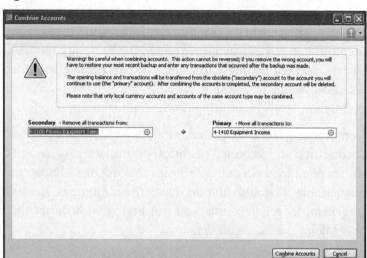

▸ The account '4-1410 Equipment Income' should be preselected as the Primary account, because it was selected in step 2. Select '4-1100 Fitness Equipment Sales' as the secondary account. Double-check that this is the correct account, as this process cannot be undone. Click the Combine Accounts button.

▸ View the Accounts List and note that '4-1100' no longer exists.

How different account levels work

The Chart of Accounts can be sorted into four hierarchical account levels, using header accounts and sequential numbering to group and subtotal like accounts. By classifying accounts according to various criteria, up to four levels of reports—ranging from Level 1, which provides a high-level overview, down to Level 4, which provides the detail—can be generated. This is useful for managers who want to view a summary of the financial reports, yet it still allows easy access to detailed reports.

Figure 7.22 shows an example of how inventory can be grouped from the data file. I have added labels to indicate the different account levels, but in reality you will not see numbering on the Accounts List. INVENTORY (1-1140) has been set up as a header account (as opposed to a detail account). Equipment Inventory (1-1410), Health Food Inventory (1-1420) and DVD Inventory (1-1430) have all been created as detail accounts. The detail accounts are indented to the right underneath the header account, and this indicates that they will be subtotalled into the header account INVENTORY.

Figure 7.22: Accounts List window: Inventory group

1-0000	Assets ◄────────────────		Level 1
1-1140	INVENTORY ◄───────		Level 2
1-1410	Equipment Inventory ◄───		Level 3
1-1420	Health Food Inventory		
1-1430	DVD Inventory		

You can move both header and detail accounts to different levels by selecting the account and clicking the Up or Down button (see figure 7.23).

Figure 7.23: Accounts List window: Up and Down buttons

8 Enter transactions using the date on which they occurred

If you paid the invoice last week but are processing it today, you still need to use last week's date when entering the transaction. This will ensure that you are producing useful and accurate information.

9 Ensure that your data file is backed up regularly

It's important to back up your data file regularly and to keep copies off-site. You should also test that you are able to restore the backed-up data file.

10 Secure your data file by setting up user passwords

Utilise the password options MYOB provides. An administrator password will allow access to the entire file, but individual passwords should be set up for all users who access the data file, including the accountant and bookkeeper. Passwords can restrict access to sections of your data and also monitor users' activities.

11 Keep personal and business spending separate

Set up separate bank and credit card accounts for your business (or, if you have more than one, for each of your businesses) as soon as practicable. Ensure that personal expenditure is kept separate and not reported as business expenditure.

12 Speak to the experts about tax issues

If you have tax-related queries, speak to the ATO, your registered tax accountant or your registered BAS agent. The business's tax obligation can be a significant burden on the business, and it's critical that you act on relevant and accurate advice.

Summary of day 7

Congratulations! You have reached the end of day 7. On this final day we have filled in a few gaps, exploring the Command Panel, the Company Data Auditor, and IAS and BAS templates. We have touched on the basic end of financial year and end of payroll year responsibilities, and we ended the day with 12 keys to staying in tiptop form as an MYOB user.

Do you recall what I said in the preface—that you don't need to understand all the mechanics and electronics of a car to be able to drive a car successfully? There is still a lot for you to learn about MYOB, but you should now feel confident to drive MYOB AccountRight in a real-life business environment.

Glossary

accrual accounting   an accounting system where income and expenditure are recognised when the transaction occurs, not when the cash is received or paid. The transaction is accrued in the accounts.

annual leave   a period of paid time off work that permanent employees are legally entitled to. In Australia most full-time employees are entitled to four weeks' annual leave after being employed for 12 months.

Australian Business Number (ABN)   the business identifier allocated by the *ATO*. All businesses should register for an ABN even though they may not be required to register for *GST*.

Australian Taxation Office (ATO)   the government's principal revenue collection agency.

bad debt   money owed to a business that is unlikely to be recovered.

Business Activity Statement (BAS)   a statement used by businesses registered for *GST* to report and pay a number of tax obligations, including *GST*, *PAYG withholding* and PAYG instalments. Business Activity Statements can be prepared on a monthly or quarterly basis.

cash accounting an accounting system where income and expenditure are recognised when the cash is received or paid.

chart of accounts a list of all the account names and numbers used in a business's *general ledger*, organised in such a way that it reflects the financial structure of the business. It serves as an index, enabling a given account to be located within the ledger.

credit an entry in the business's accounts that increases a liability, equity or income, or an entry that decreases an asset or an expense (including cost of sales). Credit appears in the right-hand column of the ledger. For every transaction, the total of all debits and credits must be equal. See also *debit*.

credit purchase a purchase made on *credit* terms; that is, where the buyer receives goods or services and agrees to pay for them at a later date on the supplier's terms.

database a large quantity of information stored in a computer and organised in a manner that facilitates retrieval.

debit an entry in the business's accounts that increases an asset or an expense (including cost of sales), or an entry that decreases a liability, equity or income. Debit appears in the left-hand column of the ledger. For every transaction, the total of all debits and credits must be equal. See also *credit*.

EMPDUPE a file produced by MYOB software that contains payroll and payment summary information for the *ATO*.

general ledger account a collection of ledger accounts into which transactions are posted in total from journals. It holds the details of business transactions of the same type—that is, transactions related to particular types of asset, liability, income, owner's equity and expense items.

GST   a tax on goods and services sold within Australia. The tax (currently 10 per cent) is collected by the provider of the good or service and remitted to the *ATO* on a quarterly basis.

Instalment Activity Statement (IAS)   a statement used by businesses to report *PAYG withholding* to the *ATO*. Instalment Activity Statements can be prepared on a monthly or quarterly basis. If a business reports *PAYG withholding* monthly and a *Business Activity Statement (BAS)* is due for the month, an IAS is not required for that month. In this example, the business would submit an IAS in February and March and a BAS in April.

inventory   a listing of items or *stock* the businesses purchases and sells.

MAPI (Messaging Application Programming Interface)   a system built into Microsoft Windows that enables different email applications to exchange emails, provided that both systems are MAPI-compliant.

microbusiness   a privately owned business with five or fewer employees.

PAYG withholding   pay as you go withholding refers to the amount a business is obliged to withhold from the salary of its employees and remit to the *ATO*.

personal leave   paid time off work on account of illness or for personal reasons (such as bereavement or illness of a family member). Personal leave is an employee entitlement, but the amount varies according to the regulations that apply to different types of employment.

reconciliation   the process of comparing financial statements such as bank accounts with the relevant ledger to ensure that they are in agreement.

small business   generally understood to be a privately owned business with fewer than 400 employees, although there is no strict definition in this sense. The *ATO* defines a small business as one with an annual turnover of less than $2 million.

stock   the items a trading business buys and sells; for example, the stock of a paint store would include cans of paint cans and rollers.

superannuation guarantee charge (SGC)   the contribution employers are legally obliged to make to the superannuation fund of almost all their employees. The current rate is 9 per cent of the employee's ordinary earnings.

trade creditor   a person or business to which a business owes money for purchases made on *credit*. Also, the name of the account used to record the amount payable.

trade debtor   a person or business that owes a business money for services or stock sold on *credit*. Also, the name of the account used to record the amount receivable.

wizard   within a computing environment, a tool that assists the user in working through tasks by presenting a series of questions or options.

Index

Also in the Learn in 7 Days series

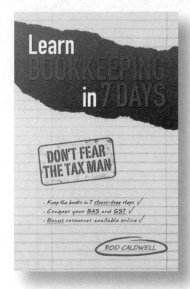

Available from all good bookstores